THE NEW WEISSENBORN METHOD FOR BASSOON

2013 Revision

Douglas E. Spaniol

Based on *Praktische Fagott-Schule mit ausfürlichen theoretischen Erläuterungen für Lehrer und Schüler*
(Practical Bassoon Method with Complete Theoretical Explanations for Teacher and Pupil)
BY JULIUS WEISSENBORN (1837-1888)

Cover Image: Bassoon Engraving from *Praktische Fagott-Schule* (1887)
Interior photographs by Dawn Pearson

With revised bibliography, additional terms, and a few modified exercises

ISBN 978-1-4234-8477-6

In Australia Contact:
Hal Leonard Australia Pty. Ltd.
4 Lentara Court
Cheltenham, Victoria, 3192 Australia
Email: ausadmin@halleonard.com.au

HAL•LEONARD®
CORPORATION

7777 W. BLUEMOUND RD. P.O. BOX 13819 MILWAUKEE, WI 53213

Visit Hal Leonard Online at **www.halleonard.com**

To my mom, who gave me my first Weissenborn Method for Bassoon
and helped me use it.

Table of Contents

Preface 6

History of the Weissenborn Method 8
    Julius Weissenborn 8
    First edition 8
    Later editions 9

A Brief History of the Bassoon 10
    Precursors to the bassoon 10
    Advent of the bassoon 11
    Almenräder and Heckel 11
    Related instruments 12
    Repertory and use 12

Parts of the Bassoon 13

Accessories 16

Care of the Bassoon 17
    Inside the case 17
    Assembly 18
    Care outside of the case 23
    Disassembly 24
    Regular maintenance 25

Reeds 26
    Sources and selection...26
    Care and maintenance 28
    Reed-adjusting tools 29
    Making adjustments 30

Producing the Tone 34
    Breathing 34
    Embouchure 35
    Tonguing and articulation...38

Posture and Hand Position 39
    Posture 39
    Left hand...42
    Left thumb in the low register 43
    Right hand...45

Selected Bibliography...47

Works Cited..48

Practical Exercises *(New notes for each lesson are enclosed in parentheses)* 49

    I (C3, D3, B2) 50

    II (E3) 52

    III (A2) 54

    IV (F3) 56

    V (G2) 58

    VI (Bb/A#2) 60

    VII (F2) 62

    VIII (Ab/G#2) 64

    IX (Eb/D#3) 66

    X (C#/Db3) 68

    XI (G3) 71

    XII.a (Gb/F#2, Gb/F#3) 74

    XII.b (A3) 76

    XIII (E2, G#/Ab3) 78

    XIV (A#/Bb3, D2) 81

    XV (B3/C4) 84

    XVI.a (Eb/D#2) 87

    XVI.b (C#/Db4) 89

    XVII (C2) 91

    XVIII.a (D4) 94

    XVIII.b (C#/Db2, B1) 97

    XIX (Bb/A#1, Eb/D#4) 99

    XX (E4, F4) 102

    XXI.a (F#/Gb4, G4) 105

    XXI.b 107

    XXII (Ab/G#4) 110

    XXIII.a (A4) 114

    XXIII.b 117

    XXIV.a 119

    XXIV.b 121

    XXIV.c 123

    XXIV.d 125

    XXIV.e 127

    XXV.a (Tenor Clef) 129

    XXV.b (Bb4) 131

    XXVI (Ornaments) 134

Major and Minor Scales in All Keys 152

Supplement

    Part I: Scale Studies 153

    Part II: Chord and Intonation Studies 160

    Part III: Finger and Trill Exercises 166

Glossary of Terms 167

Fingering Chart 170

Trill Fingerings 172

Blank Fingering Chart (for notes) 176

Music Staff Paper (for notes) 177

About the Author 179

Preface

For well over a century, students have learned to play the bassoon using Christoph Julius Weissenborn's *Praktische Fagott-Schule (Practical Bassoon-School* or *Practical Method for Bassoon)* as their primary text. Its widespread use and longevity have earned it nicknames such as "The Bassoonist's Bible" and are a testament to the quality and sound pedagogy of Weissenborn's work.

The New Weissenborn Method for Bassoon has several aims:

- To provide useful and up-to-date introductory material on performance fundamentals, and on the history, maintenance, and care of the bassoon and bassoon reeds, just as Weissenborn did in his original method.

- To focus on Weissenborn's "practical exercises" by removing extraneous materials that were appended to the method in various editions, all of which are available elsewhere.

- To make the book more easily useful for students and teachers by numbering the exercises (as Weissenborn had done originally), improving the page layout and binding, and providing additional exercises and information where needed.

- To correct errors that have appeared in previous editions, particularly in translation.

- To restore and update (where needed) Weissenborn's instructional text found within the exercises, especially indications for the use of the "speaker" or "flick" keys.

Although *The New Weissenborn Method (NWM)* is substantially different from the original method at first glance, it does contain virtually every note of Weissenborn's original, and great effort has been made to stay true to the intent of his work. Still, the deviations from Weissenborn's original work make the title *New Weissenborn Method* more appropriate than referring to this as simply a new edition. Material that was added or altered by this author is easily identifiable and includes the following:

- Each lesson begins with ready-reference information concerning the notes, techniques, and terminology introduced in that lesson.

- Additional exercises composed by this author have been added to help introduce notes.

- Most lessons have at least one duet. Where Weissenborn didn't provide one, this author added a second bassoon part to one of the exercises.

- Additional exercises from Weissenborn's *Bassoon Studies, Op. 8, No. 1* were included as necessary. This was done most often to provide additional material in keys where Weissenborn provided few or no exercises. (All 30 major and minor keys are covered in *NWM.*) In some cases, these exercises were transposed, shortened, or otherwise edited. Exercises from *Op. 8, No.1* were also used to expand the section on tenor clef.

- The scales introduced in the practical exercises have been unified so that each scale is presented in a consistent manner with regard to rhythm and articulations. Following each of these scale exercises, students are directed to the appropriate exercises in the supplement of daily scale and chord studies.

- The supplement of daily scale and chord studies has been expanded and made more user-friendly. This supplement is designed to improve not only technique, but also skills in transposing and rhythm.

- The chapter on embellishments has been restored to include all of Weissenborn's original examples, many of which do not appear in other editions. Further, explanations of the embellishments and their symbols have been updated to reflect advances in the study of performance practice that have occurred since the original publication.

The following system of octave designation is used in this book:

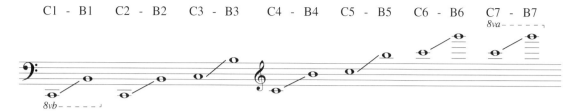

Most bassoon students do not begin their study of music by playing bassoon initially, partly due to the rather large size of the instrument. However, one should not delay the study of music simply because one is not yet ready to study the bassoon. In the introduction to his method, Weissenborn gives many pieces of sage advice regarding what bassoon students should know or study before beginning the bassoon; these are as applicable today as they were in 1887:

- Bassoon students should have several years of study "with a thorough teacher, [on] some suitable instrument, usually the violin or piano, and [the student] should try to become as proficient as possible on one or the other, better both."

- "The pupil must be able to read with ease and rapidity the bass clef, [and] must know the value of the notes and rests as well as the different kinds of meters…Learning bass clef is accomplished best and most quickly by playing the piano."

- Students should know "…intervals, by both ear and eye… the learning of the intervals and their purity requires the most practice; even the most gifted pupil, before [s]he brings this to perfection, must already have studied music with strictest diligence for some time. Correct and careful practice on the violin and the study of singing are the quickest means to this end."

- "Also, in no case is the study of harmony is to be omitted."

- "Therefore, dear pupil, *beware that thy musical education be not a one-sided one!*" (emphasis in original)

Hence, *NWM* presupposes a familiarity with bass clef and basic musical concepts and notations. If necessary, students should work with their teachers using separate materials to cover such topics.

I am greatly indebted to the late William Waterhouse for his assistance and advice in preparing this book; to Dawn Pearson of Butler University for the photographs; to Christopher Weait, Kathy Cross, and Cheri Brightman for their suggestions; and to Laura Kohrs of Hal Leonard for her outstanding work as editor.

The bassoon is an instrument unlike any other. Proper instruction on the bassoon is best provided in a one-on-one setting with a teacher who specializes in the instrument or at least is accomplished in its techniques of performance and well-versed in its repertoire. This book is intended to be an aid to such instruction and should not be seen as a substitute for private instruction by a well-qualified teacher.

Doug Spaniol
Indianapolis, Indiana, 2010

History of the Weissenborn Method[1]

Julius Weissenborn[2]

Christian Julius Weissenborn was born in Thuringia in 1837 to a musical family. His father, Johann Weissenborn (1788–1865), was a bassoonist in Thuringia. His much older brother, Friedrich Louis (1813–1862), played bassoon in the Leipzig orchestra from 1835–1855, and viola from 1855–1860. Although not the principal bassoonist, Friedrich appeared as soloist with the orchestra on eight occasions, receiving excellent reviews.[3] Like his father and brother, Julius was a successful bassoonist, achieving success at a young age. It is believed that he was playing professionally in Rostock in 1854 (age ca. 17), followed by work in St. Gallen, Eisenberg, and Düsseldorf. In 1856, at the tender age of 20, Julius began in the prestigious position of principal bassoonist of the Leipzig Gewandhaus Orchestra, with whom he appeared as soloist in 1869, 1876, and 1879. In 1882, he was appointed as the first bassoon teacher at the Royal Conservatory of Music in Leipzig. He retired from the orchestra in 1887, and passed away in 1888 at the age of 51.

In addition to his work as bassoonist and teacher, Weissenborn was highly regarded as a well-rounded musician, especially as a composer and arranger. His compositions include works for piano, wind band, orchestra, and vocal ensembles. Perhaps his most profound work is *Die Drei*, a cantata for vocal soloists, choir, and orchestra, which was premiered in Leipzig in 1874. In addition to his bassoon method, he composed two sets of bassoon etudes, a set of six bassoon trios, and 19 one-movement works for bassoon and piano. William Waterhouse surmised that the method, the two sets of etudes, and the works for bassoon and piano were conceived as a large three-part instructional set for bassoonists.

First edition

Weissenborn's method *(Praktische Fagott-Schule mit ausführlichen theoretischen Erläuterungen für Lehrer und Schüler,* or *Practical Bassoon-School with Complete Theoretical Explanations for Teacher and Pupil)* was published by Forberg in Leipzig in 1887. It begins with 18 pages of introductory text in German with an English translation set side-by-side. (The English translation was done by one Mrs. John P. Morgan. The cover states "Mrs. Morgan's translation is the only translation authorized by the author"; nonetheless, it has many instances of odd or even mistranslations.) Following the introductory material is a list of musical terms with German and English translations; a diagram of an 18-keyed bassoon with names of its parts and keys; and line-drawn pictures of a neck strap, left hand in playing position, and a reed.[4] The book also contains a fingering chart and a table of trill fingerings on separate sheets. The core of the book contains the practical exercises (organized into 25 lessons that cover 47 pages), one page on tenor clef, 11 pages on embellishments (ornaments), and an eight-page supplement containing daily scale, chord, and trill exercises. There are written explanations and annotations in both German and English found throughout the book.

---

[1] For complete information see Spaniol, Douglas E., "The History of the Weissenborn Method for Bassoon," *Celebrating Double Reeds*, ed. by T. Ewell (Baltimore, MD: International Double Reed Society, 2009), pp. 87–118.

[2] The majority of biographical information about Julius Weissenborn currently available in English is found in works written by William Waterhouse. These include the "Weissenborn" entry in *The New Grove Dictionary of Music and Musicians*, the preface to the *Bassoon Studies, Op. 8, No. 2* (Universal Edition), the liner notes for *Romanze of Weissenborn* (Equilibrium EQL 72), and, most recently, "New Light on the Weissenborn Family" *(The Double Reed*, Vol.30, No. 2). Except where noted, information in this biographical sketch is derived from these sources.

[3] Woodrow Joe Hodges, *A Biographical Dictionary of Bassoonists Born Before 1825*, 2 vols. (Ph.D. dissertation, University of Iowa, 1980), p. 653–656.

[4] In 1968, the Fox Bassoon Company (now Fox Products) of South Whitley, Indiana (U.S.A.) published a small book entitled *Der Fagott (The Bassoon)* by Julius Weisenborn (sic). The book is a reprint of the introductory materials mentioned thus far as found in Weissenborn's method.

In the introductory material, Weissenborn makes mention of bassoons pre- and post-Almenräder (see "A Brief History of the Bassoon," p. 10), citing the advantages and disadvantages of each. He specifically sings the praises of Heckel's latest advances, saying "In the last few years [more specifically since December 1885], Wilhelm Heckel…has succeeded in making a bassoon that combines all the excellencies of the old and the new. Certainly, nothing equal to it in the art of bassoon making has thus far been done." Within the lessons and the fingering charts, he does refer to fingerings and techniques that would have been necessary on earlier bassoons with fewer keys.

Later editions

Since Weissenborn's 1887 publication, three individuals have published editions of the method that have been used widely: Carl Schaefer (Forberg and Hofmeister, Germany), Fred Bettoney (Cundy-Bettoney, Boston; Cundy-Bettoney later become a division of Carl Fischer of New York), and W. F. Ambrosio (Carl Fischer).

The edition by Carl Schaefer, who was then principal bassoonist of the Leipzig Gewandhaus Orchestra and teacher at the State Conservatory in Leipzig, was published in 1920. In the foreword, Schaefer states that his main idea *("Leitmotiv")* is to "keep it short" *("kurz fassen")*. As such, Weissenborn's original eighteen pages of introductory text are reduced to three pages (still presented in German and English side-by-side). The English translation here is based on a 1903 translation by John Bernhoff, and it reads much better than the original. The diagram of the bassoon and the fingering and trill charts have been updated. The practical exercises use the same plates as the original, with small but not unimportant changes: each exercise is no longer assigned a letter, and Weissenborn's markings for use of the left thumb vent keys (also known as "flick" or "speaker" keys) are removed. There is no explanation as to why these two changes were made. References to outdated fingerings are also removed. The section on tenor clef is identical to the original; the section on embellishments has been shortened from eleven pages to seven, and the chord studies have been omitted. The supplement of scale studies is similar, though the trill exercises and some written advice have been omitted. Schaefer published updated editions with minor modifications in 1929 and 1952.

Boston bassoonist Fred Bettoney's edition was published in 1930, and was revised sometime after 1950. The 1930 edition is rarely seen, but the 1950 edition is perhaps the most popular in use in the U.S. today and is the focus of this description. The title page reads "*Method for Bassoon by Julius Weissenborn* / New Enlarged Edition Revised by Fred Bettoney." It is largely a copy of Schaefer's 1920 version, with some material drawn from Weissenborn's original edition, and some material added by Bettoney. Bettoney's edition begins with four pages of introductory text – in English only – which is derived largely from Morgan's translation, errors and all. It also includes the plate of figures (neck strap, reed, left thumb position) from Weissenborn's original, which by then were sadly outdated. The diagram of the bassoon is the one found in Schaefer's edition; in addition, the practical exercises are largely reprints of Schaefer's edition. The section on ornaments and the supplement of scale studies are identical reprints of Schaefer's version. Bettoney inserted three pages of major and minor scales with arpeggios directly before Weissenborn's practical exercises. At the end of the book, Bettoney appends scale studies by Almenräder and Milde, Weissenborn's *Fifty Advanced Studies, Op. 8 No. 2*, and the bassoon part to Weber's *Andante e Rondo Ongarese* in a version believed to be edited by Milde (although this is not mentioned). The last page is a list of musical terms with explanations in English.

"W. F. Ambrosio" is a pseudonym for Gustav Saenger (1865–1935), a New York-based violinist and conductor who served as Carl Fischer's editor-in-chief from 1907 until his death in 1935.[5] (Because bassoonists know this edition by the name Ambrosio, that name will be used here.) Ambrosio's edition was published in 1941; the title page reads *"Practical Method for the Bassoon by Julius Weissenborn /* Augmented and Adapted by W. F. Ambrosio." It begins with seven pages of introductory text covering information similar to that found in the 1887 and 1929 editions; photographs of the bassoon (with 21 keys) and its parts; and three pages of exercises covering all 15 major scales and their relative harmonic minors, each spanning one octave in the middle register of the bassoon. The musical notation of the practical exercises is essentially a reprint of the 1929 version; however, the instructional text found throughout the exercises is presented only in English (some of it reworded, although many of the errors in translation still remain). Some text has been omitted entirely. Some of the descriptions of fingerings and techniques reveal Ambrosio's lack of knowledge of the bassoon. As with the practical exercises, the sections on tenor clef and embellishments and the supplement of scale and chord studies reprint the musical notation from Schaefer, but the instructional text is presented only in English and re-worded or re-translated. After this, Ambrosio appends five pages of major and minor scales, this time covering the full range of the instrument (up to F5), one page of chromatic scale exercises, a list of musical terms, and the Weissenborn *Fifty Advanced Studies, Op. 8, No. 2.* This author's personal copy includes a fingering and trill chart dated 1924, revised 1958.

A Brief History of the Bassoon

By necessity, this essay on the history of the bassoon is decidedly short. Readers are referred to the "Bassoon" entry in *The New Grove Dictionary of Music and Musicians*[6] by William Waterhouse, or Waterhouse's *Bassoon*[7] for a more thorough treatment of the subject.

Precursors to the bassoon

The bassoon (French: *basson*, German: *Fagott*, Italian: *Fagotto*, Spanish: *fagot)* was not invented by a single person at a specific time. Reports of its being invented by Afranio degli Albonesi of Mantua, Italy, in the 16th century have proved false—his invention, the *"phagotum,"* was more a type of bagpipe and unrelated to the development of the bassoon. The confusion seems to have arisen because of the similar names (*"phagotum"* vs. *"Fagot[t]"*, each referring to the word's meaning of "a bundle of sticks").

It is difficult to detail the early history of the bassoon, due largely to a lack of evidence and confusion of terminology.[8] There is evidence of double reed instruments dating back to ancient times. If we consider these as being distant forebears of the modern bassoon, we can consider the bassoon as evolving over many, many centuries. Some of these early double reed instruments include the aulos of ancient Greece, and the rackett, shawm, and pommer of the Renaissance. The bassoon also can be seen as a descendent of non-double reed wind instruments (such as the recorder), and incorporating technologies and innovations found on such instruments (i.e., the metal bocal).

In Renaissance Europe, wind instruments often came in families or "consorts"; that is, a group of similar instruments in varying sizes and pitches (much like the family of

[5] Jeffrey Solow, "A Who's Who for Cellists," *Strings Magazine* 16:4:98 (Nov.-Dec. 2001), p. 80.
[6] William Waterhouse, "Bassoon," *The New Grove Dictionary of Music and Musicians*, ed. S. Sadie and J. Tyrrell (London: Macmillan, 2001), vol. 2, pp. 873–895.
[7] Waterhouse, *Bassoon* (London: Kahn & Averill, 2003).
[8] Waterhouse, *The New Grove Dictionary*, p. 876.

saxophones in use today). Creating a suitable bass wind instrument presented challenges due to the necessary size of the instrument relative to the size of the human body and hand. These challenges were met in various ways, including the creation of keys to open and close tone holes, and the addition of a metal bocal that could be bent. Perhaps the most important development was the doubling back of the bore upon itself, creating a hairpin shape to the bore. The immediate precursor to the bassoon is usually referred to as the "dulcian" or "curtall"; these instruments did have the doubled-back bore shape and a metal bocal, and were apparently in use from the 16th through 18th centuries.

Advent of the bassoon

The first bassoons that can be considered the earliest versions of the modern instrument appeared around the end of the 17th century. The primary difference between these instruments and the dulcians is that bassoons are made up of four wooden joints, whereas the dulcian is a single piece (hence the reference to "fagott" meaning "a bundle of sticks"). Also, bassoons normally have a range descending down to B♭1, whereas dulcians typically could only play down to C2. This necessitated the addition of a key for the low B♭, giving these earliest bassoons three keys in contrast to the typically two-keyed dulcian.

Clearly the use of the two instruments overlapped, with the bassoon gradually gaining in popularity and use until the dulcian was no longer employed. However, even the newfangled bassoon had limitations and shortcomings, most notably the inability to play all the notes of a chromatic scale.

Almenräder and Heckel

By the early 19th century, the bassoon had evolved from these early three-keyed examples to an instrument of six to nine keys. Several instrument makers, including Sax and Boehm, developed radically reformed instruments of up to 24 keys, but most of these failed to catch on with players or make a lasting impact on the development of the instrument. There are two exceptions: the French bassoonist Eugene Jancourt (1815–1901) worked with Buffet-Crampon and others to develop a 22-keyed instrument that has become the basis for the modern French *basson*.[9] The *basson* is still in use today, primarily in France. The other exception is the bassoon designed by Carl Almenräder (1786–1843).

German bassoonist Carl Almenräder is widely regarded as the most important figure in the development of the German bassoon that is in use throughout most of the world today. Working with the Schott factory and later with J.A. Heckel (1812–1877) in Biebrich, his many experiments and design ideas led to a 17-keyed instrument that could play a full chromatic scale up to B♭4. Known as the German bassoon *(Fagott)* or Heckel-system bassoon *(Heckelfagott)*, it gradually became the standard instrument for most European and North American countries, and evolved into the 22-keyed bassoon in use today. Although there were other companies manufacturing German bassoons, Heckel was well-placed as the preeminent brand well into the 20th century. Today there are many manufacturers of professional-quality German bassoons.

9 Waterhouse, *The New Grove Dictionary*, p. 884.

Related instruments

In addition to the French and German bassoons mentioned above, there are a few other bassoon-type instruments in use today. Most important of these is the contrabassoon or double bassoon. The bore of the contrabassoon is essentially twice as long as that of a bassoon; hence, it sounds one octave lower than the bassoon. Although contrabassoons were in use as early as the 17th or 18th century, nowadays it is heard most often in large orchestral works by composers of the Romantic era and later, such as Wagner, Mahler, Strauss, Stravinsky, and Schoenberg. Most professional bassoonists and serious students also learn to play the contrabassoon at some point.

There are also smaller versions of the bassoon, the tenoroon and even altoon, although these are quite rare. Some instructors use these smaller instruments for young students to begin on before switching to the bassoon.

Repertory and use

The bassoon has a long, rich history and is heard in countless pieces of music. It has been a standard member of orchestras and wind bands since the Baroque and even earlier. In the Baroque and Classical periods it was used primarily as a bass instrument, playing the same parts as the celli and basses, or serving as the bass voice of the wind section. However, composers from these periods also employed the bassoon as a melodic and even a solo instrument. Although it never lost its role as a bass instrument, it was used more and more often as a solo instrument. By the Romantic era, composers such as Tschaikovsky wrote as many solo/melodic parts for the bassoon as for the other wind instruments.

In Baroque chamber music, bassoons were often employed as a member of the continuo group, playing bass lines for other instruments' solo sonatas. However, there is a huge number of solo and trio sonatas by Telemann, Fasch, and other Baroque composers that employ the bassoon as a solo instrument. In the Classical era a pair of bassoons were found in most *Harmonie* ensembles (small chamber wind groups that featured pairs of bassoons, horns, and oboes and/or clarinets). These ensembles were very popular in the European courts of the late 18th and early 19th centuries; composers including Mozart, Haydn, and Beethoven wrote works for *Harmonie* ensembles. Of course, the bassoon is one of the five instruments of the standard woodwind quintet (flute, oboe, clarinet, bassoon, horn) that first appeared around the turn of the 19th century and has since become one of the most common chamber ensembles.

In regard to solo repertoire, the bassoon is not as well endowed as some instruments such as violin, cello, and piano; however there are many, many quality solo works for the bassoon. A few Baroque composers who wrote bassoon sonatas have already been mentioned. The most notable Baroque compositions are the 39 concertos of Antonio Vivaldi. Mozart wrote both a concerto and a sonata for bassoon, and Weber wrote two solo works for bassoon and orchestra. While it is true that there are relatively few solo works of the late 19th century, there are some fine Romantic works including those of Saint-Saëns, Elgar, and Hurlstone. Many leading composers of the 20th and early 21st centuries have composed works for solo bassoon, including Paul Hindemith, Heitor Villa-Lobos, Karlheinz Stockhausen, Luciano Berio, John Williams, and Ellen Taaffe Zwilich.

Parts of the Bassoon

The bassoon is made up of six main parts, most of which are known by two names, as indicated in Figure 1. Figure 2 shows the common names of the keys and toneholes.

- The **bell.** Most bassoons have a bell that extends the range of the instrument down to B♭1, although some have longer bells to extend the range down to A1. The top of the bell is decorated with either an ivory, imitation ivory, or metal ring (the latter is sometimes called a "French bell"). The outer surface of the bell is usually contoured; this is only decorative and does not affect the internal dimensions or bore of the instrument.

- The **long joint** or **bass joint.** There are normally six keys on this joint that control the notes of the lowest register on the bassoon. On some bassoons this joint is cut shorter (with the bell being longer as a result) so that the bassoon can fit in a smaller case.

- The **boot joint** or **butt joint.** This is the heaviest and most complex joint of the bassoon. There are two openings or sockets at the top of this joint; they show the two parts of the bore laying side-by-side. Under the metal bootcap (at the bottom of the boot joint) is a metal u-tube that connects these two parts of the bore. There is usually a hole on the boot cap for connecting the seat strap; there is also a ring near the top of the boot joint for connecting a neck strap or harness.

- The **tenor joint** or **wing joint.** This joint has the highly unusual feature of a thickened portion in the middle of the joint. This allows the three toneholes found in this portion to be drilled obliquely to accommodate the size of the human hand while still allowing the toneholes to enter the bore at the appropriate location.

- The **bocal** or **crook.** This is the thin metal tube that connects the reed to the body of the bassoon. Bocals are quite fragile and can be very expensive. The bocal has a great impact on the pitch and playing characteristics of a bassoon. A good bocal can greatly improve the quality of a bassoon, and a poor bocal can hinder the quality as well. Most professional bassoonists have several bocals to give them flexibility of pitch and the ability to better meet various playing demands.

- The **reed.** Of all the parts of the bassoon, the reed has the most profound impact on how the instrument plays. It is the vibrating body that produces the soundwaves, analogous to the strings on a string instrument or a singer's vocal cords. Reeds are made of cane from the *Arundo donax* plant. The bassoon uses a double reed; that is to say that it has two pieces of cane bound together by wires. Unlike single reed instruments, the bassoon does not have a mouthpiece in addition to the reed.

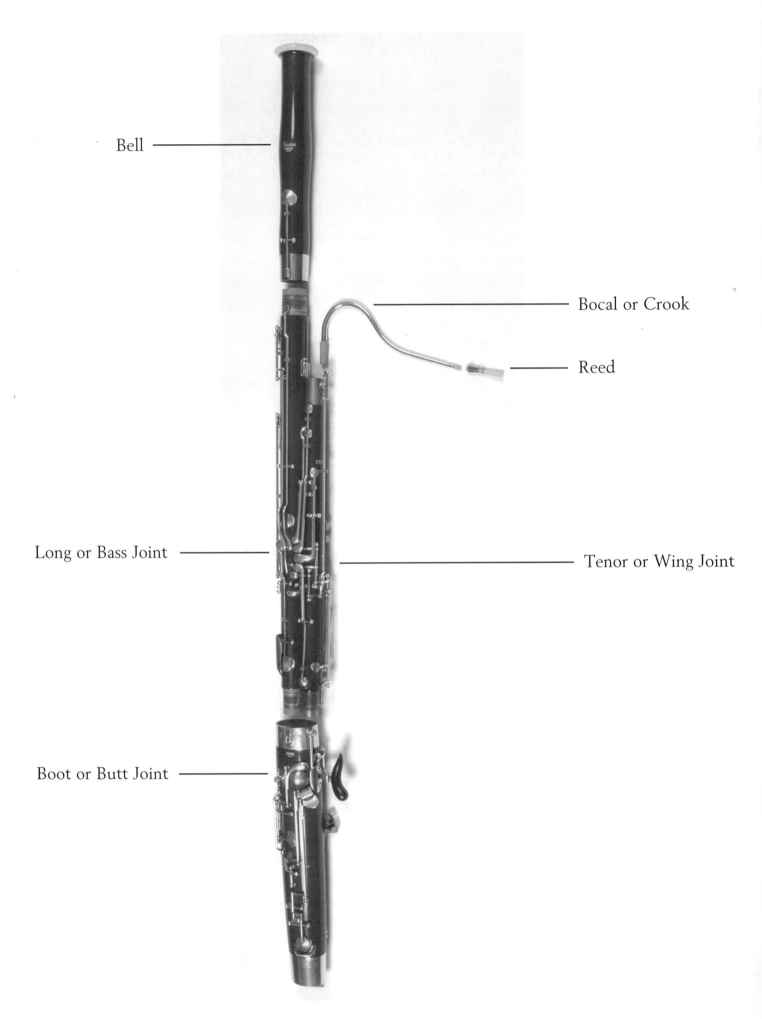

Bell

Bocal or Crook

Reed

Long or Bass Joint

Tenor or Wing Joint

Boot or Butt Joint

Fig.1. The parts of the bassoon

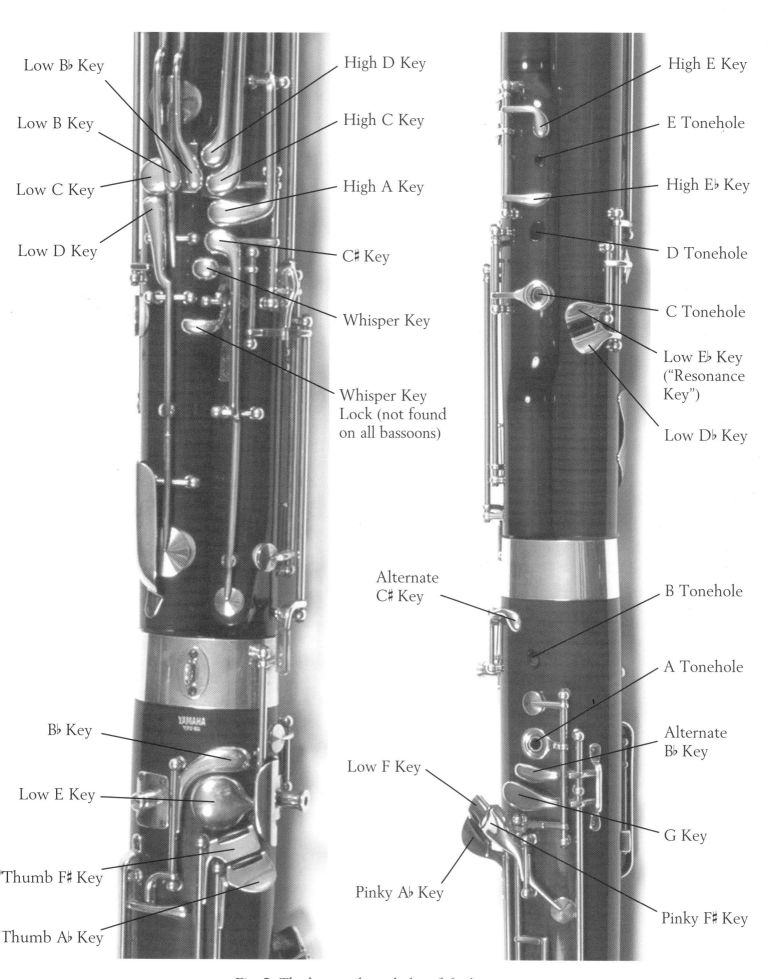

Low B♭ Key

Low B Key

Low C Key

Low D Key

High D Key

High C Key

High A Key

C♯ Key

Whisper Key

Whisper Key Lock (not found on all bassoons)

High E Key

E Tonehole

High E♭ Key

D Tonehole

C Tonehole

Low E♭ Key ("Resonance Key")

Low D♭ Key

Alternate C♯ Key

B Tonehole

A Tonehole

Alternate B♭ Key

G Key

B♭ Key

Low E Key

Thumb F♯ Key

Thumb A♭ Key

Low F Key

Pinky A♭ Key

Pinky F♯ Key

Fig. 2. The keys and toneholes of the bassoon

Accessories

Bassoonists need several accessories to be able to perform adequately and take proper care of the instrument. The list below includes recommended items that all bassoonists should keep in the case (or nearby) and have available every time the bassoon is played.

Reed case
A reed case is a handy way to store all reeds currently in use. There are many commercial reed cases available; be sure to purchase one that allows for plenty of air circulation, and that will safely hold enough reeds for your use. (Usually four to six reeds are plenty for younger bassoonists.)

Swabs
There are two basic types of swabs for bassoons – drop swabs (a.k.a. pull swabs) and push swabs. One should avoid push swabs because they do not dry the entire length of the bore, and in addition are likely to damage the instrument. Most bassoonists have two drop swabs – a smaller one for the tenor joint and a slightly larger one for the boot joint. Most importantly, the tenor and boot joints must be swabbed out *every time* the bassoon is put away after playing.

Seat strap
These are usually made of leather and come in three styles — hook, ring, and cup. To use a hook style, the cap on the bottom of the boot joint must have a small hole drilled in it. Make sure that this hole is on the side of the bassoon closest to the player. To use a ring style seat strap, adjust the ring so that it easily goes over the cap but does not touch the body of the instrument (i.e., it stays completely on the metal boot cap). Any strap should point toward the player so that the bassoon hangs on the player's right side, unimpeded by the strap.

Hand rest
Also known as a "crutch," these are usually made of black plastic or wood. The stem of the crutch attaches to the bracket next to the Low E key on the boot joint. During performance this serves as an anchor point for the right hand and helps to steady the instrument. The crutch should be positioned for maximum comfort and dexterity. There are many shapes and sizes of crutches available on the market. Many bassoonists have custom-made crutches; some bassoonists do not use a crutch at all. I recommend using one, especially for beginners, assuming that their hands are large enough.

Water container
Any small plastic container will do. Bassoon reeds *must* be soaked in water before they are played. I recommend that you not store water in your bassoon case; instead, get fresh water every time you play. This will avoid accidental water spills inside the case that could cause great damage to the instrument. Also, fresh water is more sanitary (and pleasant!) and will help your reeds last longer.

Cork grease
Any quality commercial cork grease will work. Cork grease should always be applied conservatively. Most bassoons have cork on the end of the bocal; some will have cork on the tenons (end of the joints) as well. Cork grease should not be used on tenons with string. (See "Tenons," p. 25.)

Pencil(s)
For marking music and taking notes during practice, lessons, and rehearsals.

Metronome
A wide variety of small, relatively inexpensive metronomes are available at any music store. Choose one that will fit safely in your case and has the features you desire. You should use a metronome every time you practice. Some metronomes are very advanced

and have many useful features, such as the ability to accent meters and subdivide beats. These are more expensive than other metronomes and often too large to fit in a bassoon case, but can be beneficial for practice and training. If you have such a metronome, I recommend that you have an additional, portable one that will fit in your case.

Electronic tuner

Learning to play well in tune is one the most important skills for a musician to develop. It is also one of the most difficult, especially for bassoonists. Practicing with an electronic tuner will not guarantee that you are in tune, but a tuner can be an effective aid when used wisely. There are many electronic tuners available on the market. Make sure to choose one that "hears" (picks up) the bassoon well. I also recommend purchasing a tuner that also sounds the notes of a chromatic scale. This allows one to practice tuning by ear, not just check pitches by eye.

Reed-adjusting tools

Most bassoonists learn to make their own reeds. All advanced bassoonists eventually learn to adjust their own reeds, and this often needs to be done directly before – or even during – a lesson, rehearsal, or concert. I recommend keeping the following tools (pictured in Figure 15, p. 29) in your case: mandrel, plaque, pliers, file, scraping knife, and sandpaper, plus a small screwdriver for keywork. These can be kept in a separate small pouch if there is not enough room inside the case. Further information on tools can be found in the "Reeds" section on p. 26.

Pocket music dictionary

Every musician needs to learn the many terms that are found in musical parts and scores. Develop the habit of looking up unfamiliar terms and try to memorize them as you go. Even advanced professionals occasionally come across unfamiliar terms and need to look them up.

Care of the Bassoon

Bassoons are expensive instruments. They also are quite temperamental. Well-qualified bassoon technicians are relatively scarce. Hence, it is very important for bassoonists to take good care of their instruments!

The two most common causes of damage to a bassoon are: 1) accidents that cause sudden damage, and 2) moisture that can slowly damage the instrument if it is not swabbed out after playing. Following the advice and procedures below will help reduce these risks. Of course, there is also the risk of theft that can be minimized by prudent and careful attention and through the purchase of a proper insurance policy.

Inside the case

Make sure that all parts of the bassoon (especially the bocals) are well secured when inside the case. Similarly, all accessories kept in the case must be stowed securely so that they will not rattle around loosely. In most bassoon cases, the tenor and long joints are stored next to each other, as they are when the bassoon is assembled. In such cases, a soft cloth should be kept between them. Some bassoon repair technicians recommend that the body lock (which holds the tenor and long joint together when the instrument is assembled) should be left undone while the bassoon is in the case.[10] As already mentioned, do not store reed water in your case.

There are many bassoon cases on the market today. A quality, sturdy case will protect your instrument and is well worth any added expense and weight. So called "gig-bags" are

---

[10] Richard M. Polonchak, *Primary Handbook for Bassoon* (Meredith Music Publications, 1982), p. 14.

not recommended because they may not provide enough protection. When traveling long distances with a bassoon, a sturdy hard case is essential.

A bassoon must be protected from extreme temperatures and from rapid changes in temperature. Do not leave a bassoon in a car or trunk, especially on a sunny day where the passenger compartment can heat up, or on a very cold day when both the trunk and passenger area will get very cold. The expansion and contraction of materials due to temperature change can cause a bassoon to develop leaks and other problems, and can even lead to cracking. When traveling in a car, it is best to keep the bassoon on the floor of the back seat, somewhat wedged between the front and rear seats if possible. This will protect it from extreme temperatures that may occur in a trunk, and help reduce damage in the event of an automobile accident. (However, this may not be appropriate if there are passengers in the back seat who could be injured by the bassoon case in an accident. Always use good judgement based on the situation.) If a bassoon does get cold or warm, bring it inside and allow it to return to room temperature slowly. It is especially important not to play on a cold bassoon right away. The warm air from your breath will make the inside of the instrument warm up too quickly and can lead to cracking and/or other damage.

In addition to a controlled temperature, bassoons should also be kept in a controlled-humidity environment. Ideally, the building(s) in which the bassoon is played and stored will have adequate humidity control. If not, you may want to consider using a humidifier or dehumidifier as necessary. Use of an in-the-case humidifier can also help to stabilize the bassoon. There are commercial humidifiers available or one can build one from a plastic case (such as from a cassette tape) and a sponge (Fig. 3).

Fig. 3. A homemade humidifier

Assembly

One must take adequate care to assemble the bassoon properly and thus avoid damaging the instrument. Be sure that you do not apply pressure to any of the keys or rods in such a way that they will be bent. For beginners, handling the instrument may feel awkward at first, but it soon becomes second nature. Your teacher should supervise you during assembly and disassembly until you are sure that you can do it properly and without damaging the instrument.

It is best to assemble the instrument while you are seated and with the case lying flat on the floor or safely on a chair beside you.

Begin by immersing your reed in water. The reed will then be well-soaked by the time the bassoon is assembled. Some bassoonists recommend soaking only the blades of the reed. It is better to soak the entire reed – this will help assure that the reed seals adequately on the bocal. If necessary, you can achieve this by turning the reed over halfway through the assembly process.

Although not strictly part of the assembly procedure, I recommend that students brush their teeth before playing. This will help keep the instrument clean (particularly the reed and bocal) and will help extend the usable life of the reed. If it's not possible to brush your teeth, at least rinse your mouth before playing.

Boot joint
Remove the boot joint from the case and place it on the front edge of your chair. Hold the boot joint with your left hand near the top of the joint with the thumb keys facing you (Fig. 4).

Fig. 4. Holding the boot joint   **Fig. 5.** Inserting the tenor joint

Tenor joint
Remove the tenor joint from the case. Hold it with your right hand around the middle of the joint. You may depress the thumb keys while handling the tenor joint, but be careful to not squeeze the rods that run up and down the outside of the joint. Insert the tenor joint into the smaller socket at the top of the boot joint, with the thumb keys of the tenor joint also facing you (Fig. 5). Use a slight back-and-forth twisting motion to aid insertion here and with all joints.

Rotate the tenor joint until it is properly aligned. Some bassoons have hash marks on the bottom of the tenor joint and top of the boot joint to assist in aligning. You may also check the alignment by assuring that the curved inside portion of the tenor joint is concentric to the larger socket at the top of the boot joint (Fig. 6). If not aligned properly, the linkage between the low E key and whisper key may not function properly (this will be checked near the end of the assembly process).

Fig. 6. Aligning the tenor joint   **Fig. 7.** Inserting the long joint

Long joint

Carefully lower the bassoon so that the boot is resting on the floor. Hold onto the boot joint while doing this so that it does not separate from the tenor joint and fall. Remove the long joint from the case. With the thumb keys facing you, insert the smaller end of the long joint into the remaining (larger) socket at the top of the boot joint. Hold the boot joint with your right hand, near the top of the joint; hold the long joint with your left hand near the top (Fig. 7). You may depress the Low B pad, but be sure not to bend the rod. Rotate the long joint so that the thumb keys are very near the thumb keys of the tenor joint. Most bassoons have a plate on the long joint (just below the Low Bb key) that should touch or nearly touch the small wooden portion extending from the tenor joint in this area. These are there to help assure proper alignment and prevent the two sets of thumb keys from contacting one another. If your bassoon has a body lock to secure the tenor and bass joints, you should lock it at this point (Fig. 8). If your bassoon does not have a body lock, I recommend that you have this added to your bassoon.

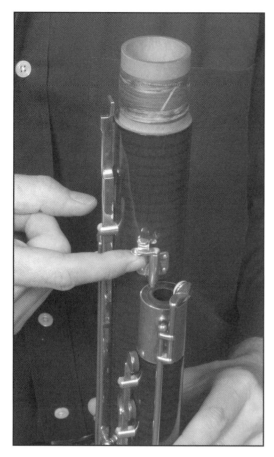

Fig. 8. Locking the body lock   **Fig. 9.** Placing the bell

Bell

Keeping your bassoon on the floor, remove the bell from the case. Depress the Low B♭ pad with your thumb and place the bell onto the long joint (Fig. 9). Rotate the bell so that the linkage between the Low B♭ pad and Low B♭ key are aligned. (Note: This is a good time to flip your reed over in the water container, if necessary.)

Seat strap and hand rest

Remove your seat strap from the case. Holding the bassoon by the boot joint, raise the bassoon and attach the seat strap to the bottom of the boot (see "Accessories," p. 16). Place the seat strap on the chair and under your thighs, with the bassoon suspended on the right side of your body and the thumb keys facing toward you. If you use a hand rest (crutch), you may insert it at this point.

Bocal

Use the utmost care when inserting the bocal. Bocals are very fragile and can be very expensive.

When handling the bocal it is best to grasp it around the bend, near the cork (Fig. 10). If your instrument has a whisper key lock, make sure that it is disengaged while inserting the bocal. Begin by applying a very thin layer of cork grease to the bocal cork to ensure that you can insert it with ease. While holding the bassoon more or less in playing position with your left hand, insert the bocal into the socket at the top of the tenor joint with your right hand. There is a ledge inside the tenor joint which allows the bocal to be inserted only a certain amount. There may or may not be cork visible above the tenor joint after the bocal is fully inserted. Some bassoonists feel that the bocal should always be inserted fully, while others feel that the bocal may be pulled out slightly to lower the pitch. Either way, be sure that the whisper key pad always covers the pinhole on the side of the bocal when the whisper key is depressed. The bocal should point toward the player's right at an angle of about 30°; this is best understood when viewed from above (Fig. 11).

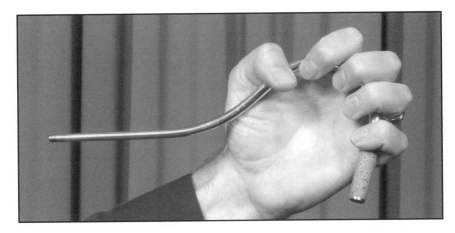

Fig.10. Grasping the bocal

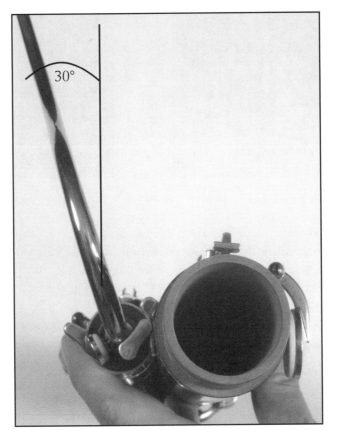

Fig.11. Angle of bocal alignment.
(bell removed for clarity)

After the bocal has been inserted, check the Low E key/whisper key linkage to assure that both keys are closing at the same time. Check this by depressing the Low E key and watching the whisper key pad. Does the whisper key close fully when the Low E key is depressed? If not, the Low E key is closing first; correct this by slightly rotating the tenor joint counterclockwise so that the thumb keys on the tenor joint are moving *away* from the thumb keys on the bass joint. (You may need to unlock the body lock in order to rotate the tenor joint.) It is also possible for the whisper key pad to close before the Low E key does. This is more difficult to determine. Again, depress the Low E key – it should feel like the pad on the Low E key contacts the body of the boot joint fully and crisply. If the whisper key closes first and you have to "push" the Low E key in order to make contact with the body of the instrument, rotate the tenor joint slightly counterclockwise so that the thumb keys on the tenor joint are moving *toward* the thumb keys on the bass joint.

Reed

By now, your reed should be well soaked and ready to play. Remove it from the water container, shaking or blowing off excess water. Place the reed firmly on the end of the bocal; here it is especially important to use a slight back-and-forth twisting motion. The reed should go on the bocal 5–8 mm and feel secure. If this is not possible, the reed may need to be reamed (see "Reeds," p. 26).

Care outside of the case

Given the size and shape of the instrument, the bassoon is particularly vulnerable to accident or damage, especially while transporting it (i.e., walking with it) outside the case. Pay particular attention to the reed and bocal, both of which are easily damaged.

When lifting or holding the instrument, always make sure that you support it from the boot joint. If you lift the instrument by the tenor/long joints – or especially by the bell – the joints may separate, causing the boot and possibly other joints to crash to the floor. Also be sure to remove and safeguard the reed and bocal while transporting the instrument or during long periods of non-use. The reed can be safely held in your lips; the bocal should be carried separately in the hand or in a bocal case or pouch. Some bassoonists place the bocal in the bell of the instrument; if you do this, take care that you do not damage the tip of the bocal or scratch the inside of the bell, and pay careful attention to avoid any accident that could damage the bocal. The bocal should *not* be placed tip-side-down into the tenor joint; the bore of the tenor joint is easily scratched, and such damage can affect tone and pitch quality.

While seated, the best resting position for the bassoon is to lean it against your right shoulder. In so doing, make sure that the reed and bocal won't hit anything that is behind you (i.e., a music stand). During long periods of rest, it is best to remove the reed and bocal. The reed can be safely held in your mouth or placed in your water cup. The bocal can be held in your hand or placed on a music stand. If you must set the bassoon down, it is best to place it in a secure bassoon stand. Avoid leaving the bassoon unattended in a rehearsal or concert space. If you must, it is best to put it back in its case. If that is not possible, at least be sure that the bassoon is in a secure stand and safe from foot traffic. You should never lay your bassoon on a chair(s), nor should you leave your reed or bocal resting on an unattended music stand where a passerby could knock them off.

One must also protect the bassoon from moisture that can cause damage to the pads and to the body of a wooden instrument. (Even though the body of a plastic instrument is not susceptible to moisture damage the way that a wooden instrument is, plastic bassoons should be cared for in the same manner.) The vast majority of wooden instruments have a lining on the inside of the tenor joint and the smaller bore of the boot joint. While the bassoon is being played, moisture accumulates in these areas and then ultimately settles into the u-tube at the bottom of the boot joint. These are the only areas of the instrument that moisture should ever be allowed to contact. Never allow the bassoon to be in a position where this moisture can run into the unlined, larger bore of the boot or up into the long joint and bell area. One must also prevent moisture from seeping into the tone holes and onto the pads. This can be achieved by always keeping the bassoon in a fairly upright position – never lay the bassoon flat or hold it in such a way that moisture will run into the toneholes or unlined portions of the bore.

Disassembly

Most damage from moisture occurs as a result of improper disassembly and storage of the instrument. Bassoonists (and their conductors, teachers, etc.) must always allow adequate time to put away the instrument properly.

Reed

Begin by removing the reed. Remove excess moisture from the inside of the reed by blowing firmly into the back end/bottom of the reed. Using your thumb and forefinger, wipe the blades from ledge to tip to remove excess moisture from the blade surface. Set your reed someplace safe (like on your music stand) and allow it to air dry for a few minutes while you put the rest of your instrument away. This will allow your reed to dry adequately before storing it (see "Reeds," p. 26).

Bocal

Grasping the bocal around the bend and using a gentle back-and-forth twisting motion, carefully remove the bocal. Make sure that the whisper key is not depressed and that the whisper key lock is not on while doing this, or you will damage the whisper key pad. Some bassoonists use a bocal swab to dry out the bocal after playing; others feel that this is unnecessary and may even damage the bocal. I've found the following procedure to be adequate: Place a finger over the pinhole in the nipple of the bocal and blow forcefully into the back end of the bocal. Carefully wipe off the tip from back to front. Place the bocal in your bassoon case, making sure that is stored and secured properly.

Bell

Remove the bell by pressing down on the Low B-flat pad and twisting back and forth. Since no moisture reaches the bell, it may be put directly into the case.

Long joint

If your bassoon has a body lock, disengage it before removing the long joint. Grasping the long joint near the top, use a slight twisting motion to remove it from the boot joint. Like the bell, the long joint should never get wet inside; hence, it may be placed directly in the case.

Tenor and boot joints

These two joints do accumulate moisture while the bassoon is being played and need to be swabbed out. Be sure to swab out the tenor and boot joints every time you put the bassoon away!

Separate the tenor joint and the boot joint, and lay the tenor joint across your lap, curved side down. (There are no toneholes along this side, so you needn't worry about moisture getting in the toneholes.) Turning your attention to the boot joint, tilt it in such a way that excess moisture runs out the smaller/lined side. *Be very careful* that moisture does not run into the larger/unlined side. Gently lower the weighted end of the boot joint's drop swab into the larger/unlined side, then tilt the boot joint so that the weight goes around the u-tube and out the smaller socket. Pull the swab through the boot joint slowly, allowing the swab time to absorb all the moisture. (This procedure should not be repeated; regularly pulling a damp swab through the unlined portion of the bore can lead to moisture damage.) Place the boot joint in the case.

Take the tenor joint off of your lap and hold it upside down. Before swabbing the tenor joint, make sure that the swab is not knotted or tangled. It is possible for a drop swab to get stuck in the tenor joint. If this happens, try to pull it out backwards. If you can't, take it to a repairman right away. Don't try to force it out – you'll only make the problem worse. After checking for knots and tangles, carefully lower the weighted end of the tenor joint's swab into the bottom of the tenor joint until it comes out the other end. Slowly pull the swab through the tenor joint. Look into the tenor joint to see if there is any moisture remaining in the bore. If so, swab again. Place the tenor joint into the case.

Reed (again) and accessories

By now, your reed should be well dried and may be placed into your reed case. Then return your accessories (hand rest, seat strap, etc.) to the case. Close and secure the case. Beware of forgetting your seat strap on the chair!

Regular maintenance

Bassoonists should also perform a few regular maintenance procedures. It is important to stress that you should only undertake those procedures for which you are qualified. Do not attempt to fix or adjust the bassoon if you are unsure of your abilities. Instead, take the bassoon to your teacher or a well-qualified repairperson. It is possible for even the most well-intentioned bassoonist to do serious damage to an instrument. Of course, this means that bassoon students should be given proper instruction in basic instrument maintenance, especially those procedures described below.

There are relatively few people who specialize in bassoon repair. Many generalists are not adequately prepared to handle the special demands presented by bassoon repair and maintenance. Oftentimes, music stores and school districts rely on ill-prepared generalists to complete their bassoon repair work. Your teacher or a nearby professional bassoonist should be able to recommend a reliable source for bassoon repair and maintenance.

Tenons

As humidity levels and temperatures change, the bassoon will expand and contract slightly. Although these changes are relatively small, they are enough to affect the grip and tension between the tenons (the narrow portions at the ends of the long joint and bottom of the tenor joint) and their receiving sockets. If the tenons are wrapped in cork, a small amount of cork grease should be applied as needed for lubrication and to keep the cork in good condition. If the tenons are wrapped in string, paraffin wax should be applied to the string instead of cork grease. Most often this is done by melting small amounts of wax and distributing this evenly around the stringed tenon. Some bassoonists achieve a similar result by rubbing solid wax on the string and then rubbing the string with a paper towel (the friction and rubbing will create enough heat to melt the wax and distribute it properly). If either cork or string tenons become loose, a small amount of plain waxed dental floss can be wrapped around them to help them seal properly in their receiving socket. This is usually needed only in winter months. If those tenons then become too tight, some or all of the floss can be removed.

Bocals

Bocals should be cleaned about once a month. Most bassoonists clean their bocals with a bocal brush; these can be purchased from any bassoon retailer. To use a bocal brush, first rinse out the bocal by running lukewarm tap water through it from back to front. Follow this by inserting the bocal brush into the back end of the bocal and carefully pushing it through the bocal until it comes out the tip. Continue pulling the bocal brush carefully until it is completely out of the bocal. Rinse the bocal again thoroughly as described above. This process may need to be repeated. Some bassoonists use a bocal swab regularly to keep their bocals clean. Other bassoonists warn against using a bocal brush or swab for fear that they could damage the bocal. As an alternative, one can clean the bocal by soaking it in warm, slightly soapy water followed by running water from the tap through the bocal to rinse it and remove debris. I would like to reiterate the value of brushing one's teeth before playing. If this is done regularly, bocals will stay relatively clean. If not, a bocal can accumulate a rather surprising collection of debris!

Pads

Occasionally the pads of the bassoon will become sticky, causing them to be noisy or causing the key to open late or not at all. To clean a sticky pad, insert a piece of ordinary, clean white paper under the pad, then swipe the pad with the paper while holding the pad closed. This may need to be repeated several times. If the pad is still sticky it may need to be cleaned or replaced by a repairperson.

Annual service

Bassoons should be serviced annually by a well-qualified repairperson. This service should include:

- sealing any leaks in the instrument
- replacing pads as needed
- cleaning and oiling the keywork
- adjusting key heights and tensions
- other repair and maintenance as recommended by the repairperson

An advanced bassoonist would be well advised to learn to do some or even all of these things by her- or himself, but again, one should not attempt such things unless properly trained and prepared.

Reeds

One cannot overemphasize the importance of the reed to the bassoon and to bassoon players. The reed is the vibrating body that produces the sound waves. Aside from the player herself, the reed is the most important factor in determining the pitch, timbre, and other characteristics of the bassoon sound.

The bassoon is, of course, a double reed instrument, meaning that the reed is made of two pieces of cane bound together. The cane used for bassoon reeds is derived from the plant *Arundo donax*, a plant that looks similar to bamboo and grows in swampy areas. Most reed cane comes from southern France, although today one can buy cane from many other parts of the world. Reeds made from synthetic materials are sometimes used by beginners; attempts to make a professional quality synthetic reed have thus far met with approval from only a very small minority of professional bassoonists.

There are several books and sources of information available on the topic of reed-making and adjusting (see "Selected Bibliography," pp. 47–48). A complete discussion of this topic is beyond the scope of this book; however, some basic information on reed adjusting is found on p. 30 ("Making adjustments").

Sources and selection

Virtually all professional or advanced bassoonists have learned to make reeds, and the majority of these bassoonists perform on self-made reeds exclusively, or nearly so. Some bassoonists rely on reeds hand-made by professional reed makers. The quality of commercially produced reeds has improved dramatically in recent years; some professional bassoonists now find such reeds satisfactory for their own use. Whatever source of reeds a professional bassoonist may eventually settle upon, she or he most certainly will make adjustments to suit their own taste and to maintain the reed's performance.

Younger bassoonists who are not yet proficient at making and/or adjusting reeds face the problem of finding a supply of adequate reeds. This is one reason why it so crucial for young bassoonists to have a well-qualified private teacher. Such a teacher will be able to ensure that her or his students have decent reeds to play on. The teacher may achieve this by making reeds for the student, keeping a supply of reeds from a satisfactory source that the students may then purchase from the teacher, or directing students to an outside source of satisfactory reeds. Often some combination of these three is used. Whatever the source of reeds, a well-qualified teacher will be able to adjust reeds to suit students' needs, preferences, and abilities. Eventually serious bassoon students learn to adjust and make their own reeds. At what point this should happen is open to discussion; a good teacher will provide quality instruction in these areas at an appropriate point in the student's course of study.

If you have the opportunity to select a few reeds for purchase from a wide assortment, look for the following characteristics in addition to (or in lieu of) a playing test:

- The reed should be free of cracks or other obvious defects.
- The back end of the reed should be completely circular with no indication whatsoever of an elliptical shape. The reed should go on the bocal 5–8 mm and should fit snugly. These qualities will help insure an airtight seal between the reed and bocal.
- The wires of the reed should be placed properly. Christopher Weait recommends that wires be placed at 5, 19, and 27 mms from the back of the reed.[11] They should also be straight and fairly snug. If one is proficient at adjusting reed wires (see "Making adjustments," p. 30), this is less of a concern.
- The surface of the reed blades should be fairly smooth to the touch.
- The tip opening should have a characteristic bow shape and should be symmetrical side-to-side and blade-to-blade (see Fig. 12).
- The blades should gradually taper from the back of the spine to the corners of the tip. This can best be checked by holding the reed up to a strong light source; the patterns of light and dark areas will reveal the relative thickness of the blade. Look for the characteristic "thumbnail" pattern as seen in Figure 13. This pattern should also be symmetrical side-to-side and blade-to-blade.

Fig. 12. Tip opening with characteristic bow shape

---

[11] Christopher Weait, *Bassoon Reed-Making: An Illustrated Basic Method* (Worthington, OH: Christopher Weait, 2008), p. 2.

Fig.13. Characteristic "thumbnail" pattern of reed

Care and maintenance

Keeping an adequate supply of good reeds is an ongoing challenge for all bassoonists, often resulting in considerable expense and anxiety. It makes sense to take good care of the reeds we have to minimize these issues.

Reeds have a limited life span that can come to an end due to accident or due to a reed simply wearing out. To avoid accidents, reeds should be kept safe in a reed case, well-soaked before playing or adjusting, safeguarded while in use, and treated with great care while they are being worked on. To extend their useful lifespan before they wear out, do the following:

- Keep reeds dry when not in use. A good reed case will provide adequate air circulation. Keeping the reed case open and out of the bassoon case when appropriate will further aid the drying process.

- Soak reeds in clean water only. Don't reuse water from a previous day, rehearsal, etc. (Remember not to store water in your case.)

- Rotate your reeds, i.e., use one reed one day, a different reed the following day. This will allow the reeds to dry thoroughly and "rest" between uses. It will also assure that you are not dependent on just one reed. I suggest having at least four good reeds in your rotation at all times.

- Rinse off reeds and dry them before storing (see "Disassembly," p. 24).

- Periodically clean your reeds by running a strong stream of water from the tap through them from back to front. You may aid this process by carefully drawing a soft pipe cleaner through the reed – also from back to front – and using a slight side-to-side motion to wipe the entire blade surface (Fig. 14).

- Reeds may be further cleaned and disinfected by soaking in a 3% hydrogen peroxide solution for five to ten minutes, followed by rinsing and cleaning in the above manner. (Note: some bassoonists warn against using peroxide claiming that it alters the cane itself.)

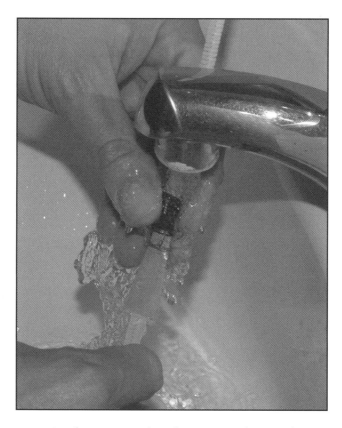

Fig.14. Cleaning reed with water and pipe cleaner

Reed-adjusting tools

As mentioned earlier, a complete discussion of reed adjusting is beyond the scope of this book. (For a more thorough discussion, see the books on reed-making listed in the Selected Bibliography.) There are a few easy adjustments, though, that bassoonists should learn relatively early in their education. Figure 15 shows tools needed for these adjustments; information about each tool is provided on p. 30. Most of these tools are available from any bassoon retailer; some can also be purchased at general music retailers, hardware stores, or even general merchandise stores.

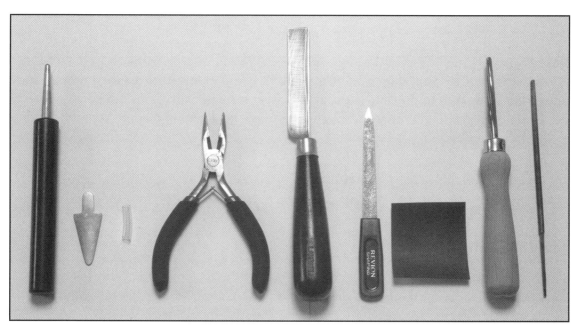

Fig 15. From left to right: mandrel, plaque, "iron", pliers, scraping knife, flat file, sandpaper, reamer, rat tile file

Mandrel (Short)

A mandrel is a hand tool that is used to hold the reed while it is being worked on. (Note: be sure to buy a regular mandrel, not a long or forming mandrel.)

Plaque

A plaque is a small piece of metal, wood, or plastic that is placed between the blades of the reed to give support when trimming the blades. Be careful when inserting and removing a plaque so as not to damage the reed. When working on a reed with an inserted plaque, always keep one finger under the bottom blade to support it (Fig. 22).

Iron

A reed "iron" is a little-known, little-used bassoon tool—you probably won't find one in any supplier's catalog. An iron is used to smooth out the blades. A reed iron can be made out of many things. I recommend a short (ca. 1") piece of plastic tubing, such as the kind used for fish tank filter systems.

Pliers

Pliers have several uses in reed making and adjustment. They are used to tighten loose wires, as well as to adjust the shape and size of the tip opening and/or the tube. I recommend small, snub nose pliers with built-in wire cutters. It helps if they are also spring loaded and have grooves on the jaws.

Scraping knife

A scraping knife is used to thin the blades of the reed. It should be a quality, precision tool and should be well cared for. A wide variety of knives are available from reed suppliers. I recommend a double-hollow ground knife.

Flat file

There are many types of flat files available and in use by bassoonists today. Any small (ca. 4") flat file will do as long as it doesn't have just one set of parallel grooves; it should have crisscrossing grooves, or some other complex pattern. One of the best (as well as cheapest) is a small metal nail file (not an emery board). In addition to being inexpensive, these usually come with a "shaping" (coarser) side and "finishing" (less coarse) side.

Sandpaper

Used to sand blades and other surfaces, this must be wet/dry sandpaper. Buy 600 grit (and possibly finer grits as well) and cut into small squares (approximately 1" x 2"). Before using, rub the backs of these pieces against a sharp table edge, which will break the paper backing and make the sandpaper more flexible.

Reamer

A reamer is used to form, shape, or enlarge the butt end of a reed to assure a proper fit on the bocal. Be sure to purchase a quality reamer, as low-quality ones can be counterproductive. I recommend multi-fluted, spiral ground, or diamond reamers; reamers with a straight single flute should be avoided.

Rat tail file

Used for smoothing out the inside of the tube and for removing any loose fibers, especially after reaming. Buy a small, round file (approximately 4").

Making adjustments

The adjustments explained in this section are ones that bassoonists can learn relatively early in their education. If a reed is unsatisfactory, I recommend that the following adjustments be made as needed in the order given.

Sealing a reed that leaks on the bocal

To play well, reeds must form an airtight seal on the bocal. To test this, take the reed and bocal off the bassoon. With the reed on the bocal, plug up the open end of the bocal with the left thumb and the small pinhole with the right thumb. Blow into the reed. If you feel, hear, or see air escaping (in the form of bubbles or moisture splattering), the seal needs to be corrected. Use the following procedures in the order listed, testing the seal after each one:

1) Push the reed further onto the bocal.

2) Soak the back end of the reed in water for another minute or two. Replace reed on bocal, assuring that the reed is on all the way.

3) If the reed is going on the bocal less than 5-8mm and/or the reed is wobbly on the bocal, it needs to be reamed. To ream a reed, insert the reamer in the back end and gently twist. Stop often to re-check the seal and to wipe the shavings off of the reamer. If the inner surface is rough or there are loose fibers inside the reed, file the inside with the rat tail file.

4) If the reed is still leaking, place an additional wire as near the back end of the reed as possible (Fig. 16). To do this, place the reed on the mandrel, wrap a piece of 22 gauge brass wire around this part of the reed twisting the ends together, and tighten with pliers. If necessary, ream the reed again. Although not often necessary, this procedure will assure an airtight seal on virtually all reeds.

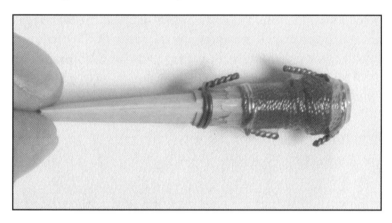

Fig 16. Reed with added fourth wire at back (to help seal the reed on the bocal)

Adjusting placement and tension of wires
As mentioned earlier, the wires of the reed should be placed at or close to 5, 19, and 27 mms from the back of the reed for most reed styles. (Some reed styles will vary significantly from these measurements.) The wires should also be straight and have the proper tension (snugness) against the reed.

To tighten a wire, place the reed on the mandrel and bend the twisted end upward so that it is pointing directly away from the reed. With pliers, grab the twist and pull somewhat firmly away from the reed and mandrel (Fig. 17). You should feel and see the wire tightening. Twist the wire in the direction already twisted to hold the tension. Bend the twist back down to its original position.

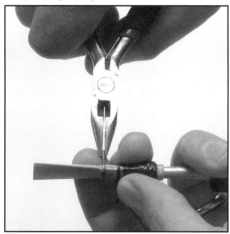

Fig.17. Tightening a wire with pliers

To loosen a wire, do as above but push the pliers towards the reed and mandrel and untwist the wire.

To adjust a wire's position, first loosen the wire (if necessary) as described above, then move the wire to its desired position using your fingertips or fingernails. Lastly, tighten the wire as above to keep it in its new, desired position.

The back wire (5mm from the back of the reed) is most often under the wrapping and inaccessible, and is ideally put on very tightly. Hence, bassoonists generally do not adjust this wire.

The middle wire (at 19mm) should be just snug enough that you can't move it with your fingertips or fingernails. Don't overtighten so that it cinches the reed leaving easily visible indentations in the bark. Moving the middle wire toward the back of the reed will normally result in a darker tone; moving it toward the tip of the reed will normally create a brighter sound.

The blade wire (at 27mm) should be snug enough that it will stay in place, but not so tight that you can't move it fairly easily with your fingertips or nails. If this wire is too tight, the reed will probably have a pinched sound and feel, and the low register will be hampered. If it is too loose, the sound may be unfocused, and the high register may suffer. Moving this wire toward the tip will raise the overall pitch of the reed, focus the sound, and improve the high register/hinder the lower register. Moving this wire down toward the back of the reed will have the opposite effect: a lower pitch, a less focused sound, and an improved low register/hindered upper register.

Adjusting the tip opening by squeezing the wires
These adjustments can have a very profound effect on the way a reed plays. Fortunately, they are reversible.

The chart below shows the playing characteristics of a reed as the tip changes from being more closed to more open:

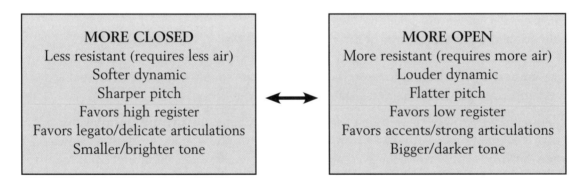

MORE CLOSED	MORE OPEN
Less resistant (requires less air)	More resistant (requires more air)
Softer dynamic	Louder dynamic
Sharper pitch	Flatter pitch
Favors high register	Favors low register
Favors legato/delicate articulations	Favors accents/strong articulations
Smaller/brighter tone	Bigger/darker tone

To adjust the opening of the tip, first make sure that the reed is well soaked. Place the reed on the mandrel during adjustments and be sure to watch the tip as it opens and closes. If you open the tip too far, one or both blades will crack!

- To open the tip: using pliers, squeeze the blade wire from the sides (Fig. 18) and/or squeeze the middle wire from the top and bottom (Fig. 19).
- To close the tip: using pliers, squeeze the blade wire from the top and bottom (Fig. 20) and/or squeeze the middle wire from the sides (Fig. 21).

Which wire should be adjusted? There isn't a short answer to this. Rather, the following points should be kept in mind:

- The blade wire has a substantial effect on the tip opening, while the middle wire has a more subtle effect on the tip opening.
- The middle wire should be close to circular; that is, it should be just slightly oval, slightly wider than it is tall.
- The blade wire should be somewhat flatter (more oval) than the middle wire.
- Squeezing the middle wire from the sides will increase the arch of the reed tip resulting in a darker sound; squeezing it from the top and bottom will decrease this arch resulting in a brighter sound.

Fig. 18. Opening tip by squeezing sides of blade wire

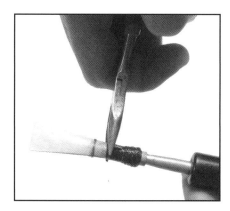

Fig. 19. Opening tip by squeezing top and bottom of middle wire

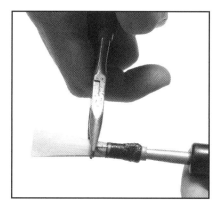

Fig. 20. Closing tip by squeezing top and bottom of blade wire

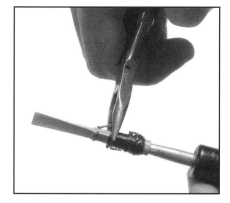

Fig. 21. Closing tip by squeezing sides of middle wire

"Ironing" the Reed

This is a relatively little-known adjustment, but is advocated by Christopher Weait in his reed-making book.[12] Ironing a reed makes no substantial change in the appearance or make-up of the reed; it simply helps it to play its best. This is especially noticeable in the day-to-day changes that reeds undergo – one day, a reed will play well; the next day, it can feel like a different reed. Ironing reeds will help minimize this effect.

To iron a reed, first soak it well. Place it on a mandrel and carefully insert a plaque between the blades of the reed. Always keep a finger under the bottom blade of the reed to support it! If you don't do this, the bottom blade is likely to crack. With your reed iron, gently but firmly rub the reed from the shoulder towards the tip, going clear off the tip (Fig. 22). Do this for the entire width of the reed so that the whole blade surface gets ironed. Turn the reed over and do the same on the other blade. After ironing, play the reed again. Ideally, it will now play its best.

---

[12] Weait, *op. cit.*, p. 31.

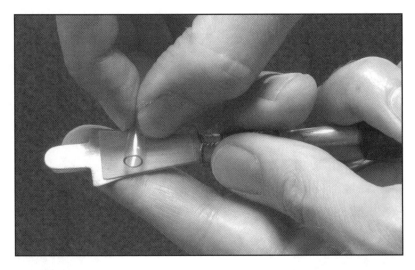

Fig.22. "Ironing" a reed (note finger under plaque for support)

Adjusting reeds by thinning the blades

These types of adjustments take years to master and are the focus of most discussions about reed making and adjusting. Young bassoonists should work with their teacher to develop proper techniques for thinning the blades using scraping knives, files, and/or sandpaper. Learning to thin the tip can be especially useful, and generally has a low risk of worsening the reed's performance. The reed-making books in the Selected Bibliography can also be a good source of learning how to use these tools and where to scrape on the blades.

Producing the Tone

The ability to produce and control the tone of the bassoon is the most difficult aspect of bassoon performance to master, and the most important in determining one's success as a bassoonist – much more so than the ability to move one's fingers and tongue rapidly. Bassoonists continually strive to produce a pleasant timbre, to play well in tune at all dynamics, and to begin and end notes well.

This section will provide some introductory information and guidelines. Please keep in mind the limitations of describing such subtle and complicated processes in writing. Also keep in mind that most of the mechanics of producing the bassoon tone are invisible to the eye. We cannot see the air flowing through the reed, the reed vibrating, the tongue moving, etc. Hence a bassoon student must work with a teacher who can assess the student's use of embouchure, air, and tongue; provide adequate demonstrations and a good model for the student to imitate; and instruct the student in practice techniques and exercises to improve these aspects of bassoon performance. Again, the importance of private study with a well-qualified teacher cannot be overstated, especially in regard to this topic.

Breathing

The breath makes the reed vibrate, hence the breath is analogous to the string player's bow. And just as good string players work long and hard to master bow technique, bassoonists must strive to master breath technique. String players have an advantage in that they can see their bow, plus the bows of their teachers and colleagues. The bassoonist's task is complicated by the fact we cannot see our breath. Visualizing a good string player's bow may help bassoonists, as may observing skilled bassoonists' posture and body use in performance.

Bassoonists should develop the ability to use their full breath capacity. That is, bassoonists should learn to inhale fully and learn to play until their breath capacity is completely exhausted. (I like to think of this as "filling the tank all the way to full" and playing "until the gauge is on empty".) To inhale fully, one should expand the torso as much as possible, including both the abdominal area and the rib cage area. The shoulders do not need to be raised; they should be left in a relaxed, lowered position. To exhale fully, one needs to do the opposite: contract the torso as much as possible. As one nears the end of one's breath, this requires more and more effort.

In performance, one primarily uses the abdominal muscles to control the exhalation of air. It is advisable to contract these abdominal muscles first, leaving the rib cage expanded and somewhat still. When necessary, one then contracts the rib cage area to exhale remaining air. The amount of air exhaled, and the speed or pressure with which it is exhaled, will affect the volume, tone, and pitch of the sound. A greater amount of air will result in a louder, fuller sound. A faster air stream will result in a higher pitch. Generally speaking, one uses a slower, wider air stream for the lower registers, and a faster, narrower air stream for higher registers.

Perhaps most importantly, bassoonists should breathe freely and comfortably. Playing the bassoon well requires a certain amount of energy in the air stream, but this doesn't mean that bassoonists need to struggle or "force" the air. The bassoon itself provides a certain amount of resistance. Feel that resistance and blow into it; don't add to it.

Embouchure

To most people, the term "embouchure" applies to the position and use of the lips. For our purposes here, I'd like to expand this definition to include the oral cavity (mouth) and the throat. These three mechanisms have a profound impact on the pitch, timbre, and dynamic of the bassoon.

Lips

The bassoonist's lips should normally be kept relaxed and in a relatively natural, comfortable position. Both the top and bottom lip should be rolled over the teeth slightly. Normally some of the lip is still visible when playing; that is, do not roll your lips under so much that the lips disappear from view completely. The lips should form a shape as if saying "oh" or "ooh", with the corners pushed in slightly (Fig. 25a). Think of the lips gently closing around the reed like a drawstring with equal pressure all around. Avoid pulling the corners back as when smiling, and applying pressure on the reed from above and below only (Fig. 25b). Except when playing in the higher registers, the pressure on the reed from the embouchure should be very slight – just enough to direct the air into the reed without leaking around the sides. Think of keeping the reed as open as possible; don't close it with embouchure pressure. When playing in higher registers, increased pressure to close the reed is sometimes necessary.

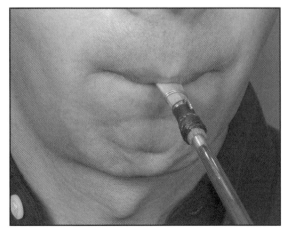
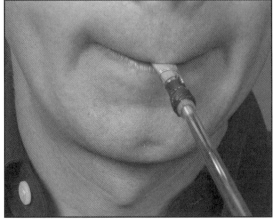

| **Fig. 25a.** A good bassoon embouchure | **Fig. 25b.** Embouchure with corners pulled back |

The amount of reed put in the mouth has a major impact on tone and pitch. For normal playing, the lips should be positioned near the center of the reed blades, slightly closer to the shoulder/blade wire than to the tip (Fig.26). The top lip should be slightly closer to the shoulder than the bottom lip is, reflecting the natural human overbite. Experiment with the amount of reed in the mouth to find the position that gives the best tone and pitch. Putting less reed in the mouth will lower the pitch, improve the lower registers, and may make rapid tonguing easier (Fig 27). Putting more reed in the mouth raises the pitch and makes it easier to play in the higher registers (Fig. 28). These variations will also affect the timbre; the differences are best observed through experimentation.

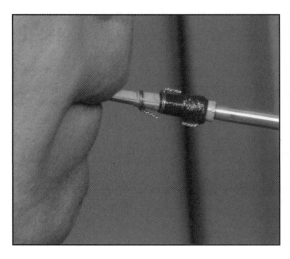 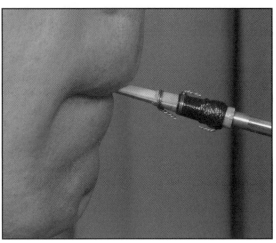

Fig. 26. Typical amount of reed in mouth   **Fig. 27.** Less reed in mouth

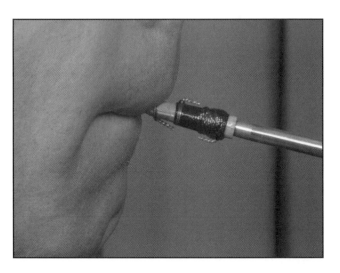

Fig. 28. More reed in mouth

Angle of Reed Entry
The angle at which the reed enters the mouth has a very pronounced impact on the overall pitch, as well as the timbre of the instrument. A typical angle is shown in Figure 29. If the reed comes into the mouth from above, the pitch will be sharper and the tone more pinched (Fig. 30). A reed that enters the mouth more from below will have a lower pitch and a less focused tone (Fig. 31). Adjusting this angle will require that the bassoon be repositioned and/or that a different shape of bocal be used. The typical North American bocal may lead one to play with the reed entering the mouth from above as in Figure 30. Some bocal manufacturers offer bocals in more than one shape. (See Figure 32 for various shapes of bocals.)

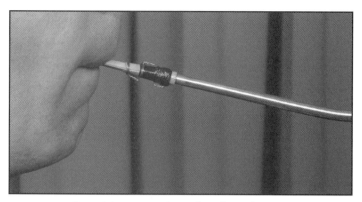

Fig. 29. Typical angle of reed entry

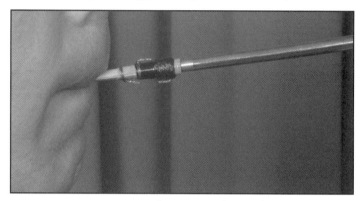

Fig. 30. Reed entering from above

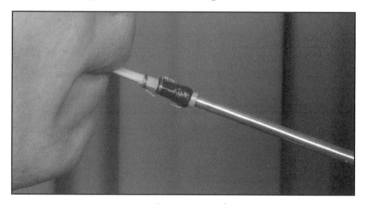

Fig. 31. Reed entering from below

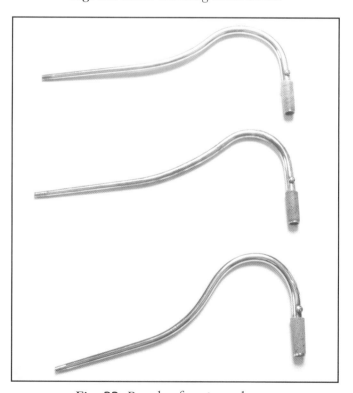

Fig. 32. Bocals of various shapes

Oral cavity

The shape and position of the oral cavity (the inside of the mouth) also has a profound impact on tone and pitch. To control this, it is best to think of the vowel sound that one is forming while playing. Vowel sounds can be thought of in a continuum from open to closed. The chart below shows this continuum, along with the effects on tone:

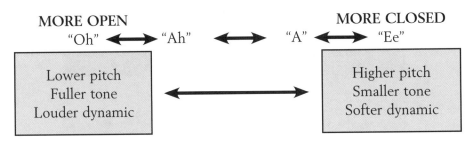

You will notice that as you move from an open oral cavity to a closed oral cavity, the tongue lifts and comes closer to the roof of the mouth.

Throat

The throat generally works in conjunction with the oral cavity. In other words, as the oral cavity moves to a more open position, so does the throat. A bassoonist should be aware of the position and use of the muscles of the throat and engage them just as one does the tongue in the oral cavity.

Each register – indeed each note – of the bassoon responds uniquely. The air, oral cavity, and throat work together to produce the desired tone, pitch, and dynamic of each note. With effective practice and teaching, these mechanisms work together almost unconsciously during performance, just as your tongue, lips, throat, and respiratory systems work almost unconsciously during speech. Your goal should be to train yourself to play bassoon such that, you can sing or think the sound in your head and that these mechanisms will automatically work together to produce the sounds that you hear internally.

Tonguing and articulation

It's important to note that it is the air that makes the reed vibrate. The tongue stops the reed from vibrating.

The tongue should touch the very tip of the reed. Sometimes it is helpful to think of the tongue touching only the bottom blade of the reed. The tip of the reed should contact the top side of the tongue, as close to the tip of the tongue as possible. The first note of a piece, or the first note after a rest or breath, will nearly always "begin with the tongue" – what this really means is that the note will begin when we remove the tongue from the reed, allowing the air to go through the reed and make it vibrate, as in saying "toh" or "tah." To begin a note in this manner, one should set the fingering and embouchure, place the tip of the tongue on the tip of the reed, and build the requisite air pressure. Then, when the tongue is removed from the reed, the note will begin. With experience and practice, one learns to do this very quickly and automatically.

There is a general misconception that the tongue moves forward and back when tonguing. It is closer to the truth to say that the tip of the tongue moves up and down when tonguing. Say "ta" quickly and repeatedly, and note the motion of your tongue. Observe this in a mirror if possible.

Most difficulties in tonguing are caused by contacting the reed too far back on the tongue and/or moving the tongue too far. One should strive to move only the tip of the tongue, tapping the reed lightly from below, and to move the tongue the smallest distance possible. This, coupled with good use of the air and embouchure, will facilitate rapid tonguing with a good tone at the start of the note.

Occasionally one ends a note by returning the tongue to the reed, as in saying "tot." This will create a very sudden ending to a note. More often, a note is ended "with the air" as in saying "toh" or "tah." It can be quite difficult to learn to end a note well this way. Oftentimes, the pitch or tone will change at the end of the note. Again, with careful practice and quality instruction, one can learn to master this.

Playing on the reed and bocal only (the "bocalphone," as shown in Lesson I) is an excellent way to learn, develop, and teach fundamentals of tone production. This is true for beginners as well as advanced players, and all bassoonists in between.

The various types of articulations – that is, the way notes are started and ended – are covered fully in the "Practical Exercises" portion of this book.

Posture and Hand Position

Posture

The bassoon is a relatively large, heavy instrument. This can create difficulties in finding a comfortable position and efficient ergonomics while playing. It is advised that beginning bassoonists learn to play seated, using a seat strap to support the instrument. Playing while standing can be helpful in practicing bassoon, and in some performance situations; however, this should not be attempted too early in one's development as a bassoonist.

Bassoonists do require a proper chair to perform in. This means a chair without arms, with a seat that is not too wide and that does not slope towards the back. Some bassoonists place blocks under the back legs to assure that the seat is level or even leaning forward slightly.

While playing the bassoon, one should strive to keep their muscles relaxed and free. Avoid excess tension and rigidity that can hamper technique and lead to medical problems. Keep all joints as close as possible to their "neutral position" – the point where the joint is neither flexed nor extended, and where both sets of muscles controlling the joint are relaxed. As an example, see the wrist in various positions in Figures 33–35.

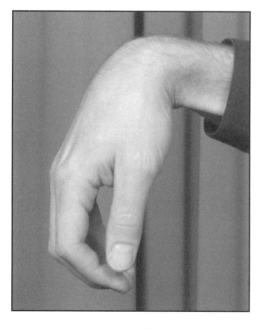

Fig. 33. Wrist flexed

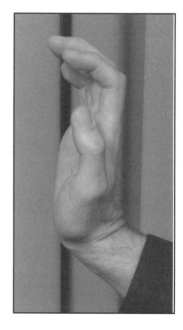

Fig. 34. Wrist extended

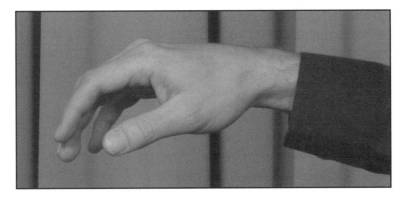

Fig. 35. Wrist in neutral position

When playing bassoon, one should sit with "good posture." This means that one should sit in a way that is relaxed, comfortable, and flexible, and that allows effective use of the body. To achieve this, it is best to first sit in a chair without the bassoon. Do not allow your hips to roll backwards, thereby creating a curvature in the lower spine that collapses the abdomen (Fig. 36). Rather, keep the hips and spine aligned by sitting on the back of the thighs. Keep the head as far away from the waist as possible without straining. This will allow for maximum expansion and contraction of the torso (hence, maximum air supply) and effective use of the respiratory system and upper extremities (Fig. 37). In most cases, it is best to sit near the back of the chair, but not leaning against the chair back (if there is one).

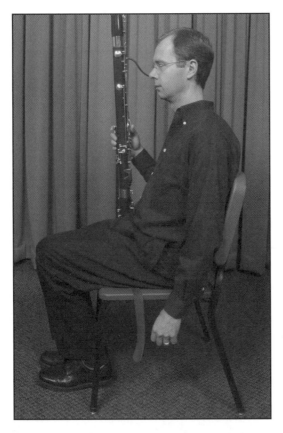
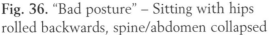

Fig. 36. "Bad posture" – Sitting with hips rolled backwards, spine/abdomen collapsed

Fig. 37. "Good posture" – Sitting on the back of the thighs, head/spine aligned

In playing position, the bassoon will hang by the seat strap on the player's right side. It will lean forward as well as crossing from right to left in front of the player's torso; that is, the bell will point somewhat forward and to the player's left. The bassoon normally leans against a player's right thigh at a point that acts somewhat like a fulcrum. The left hand should be directly in front of the sternum (or nearly so) and will support some of the weight of the instrument. Maintaining this good sitting position in a proper chair, put the bassoon in playing position while keeping this fundamental rule in mind: "Let the bassoon come to you; don't go to the bassoon." Holding the bassoon with your left hand around the wing and long joints, pull the bassoon toward you. The reed should come directly to your lips. If it is too low, raise the bassoon by pulling down on the loose end of the seat strap. If it is too high, lower the bassoon by adjusting the seat strap accordingly (Figs. 38 and 39).

Fig. 38. Playing position – side view   **Fig. 39.** Playing position – front view

The position of the bassoon can also be altered by moving it and the seat strap closer to the front or back of the chair. In most cases it is best to have the bassoon near the front of the chair and the player's hips near the back, as in Figure 40. This will help keep the bassoon more upright, thereby reducing the weight on the left hand. It will also help prevent the player's right shoulder from being positioned unnaturally back, and will prevent the right wrist from being bent too sharply, as in Figure 41. The shape or bend of the bocal will in part determine this position (Fig. 32).

Fig. 40. Bassoon near front of chair   **Fig. 41.** Bassoon near back of chair

Note that in Figure 40 the bassoon is close to vertical, the right shoulder is aligned, and the right wrist is near the neutral position. In Figure 41 the bassoon is tilted, the right shoulder is pushed back, and the right wrist is flexed.

Minor adjustments to the playing position can be made by repositioning the bocal slightly to the left or right. Make sure that the whisper key still closes the pinhole on the bocal. Lastly, twist the reed so that it is horizontal when the bassoon is in playing position.

Left hand

This book will use the following system (which is common among bassoonists) for numbering fingers: index finger = 1; middle finger = 2, ring finger = 3, pinky = 4; the thumb is sometimes referred to as 5, but more often simply called "thumb." Fingers on the right hand will be abbreviated RH1, RH2, etc.; the left hand will be LH1, LH2, etc.

The "home position" of the left hand has the index finger over the first tone hole on the wing joint; the middle finger over the second tone hole, and the ring finger over the third. Some bassoons have a key over the third tone hole to reduce the stretch between the second and third fingers; this is very helpful, especially for players with smaller hands. The pinky rests lightly upon or directly over the Low E♭ key ("resonance" key) (Fig. 42). Note that the fingers here are slightly curved and that the keys and tone holes are being touched by the fleshy part of the fingertips. Avoid collapsing the third knuckles of the fingers; this will hamper technique (Fig. 43).

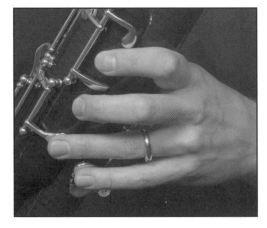

Fig. 42. Left hand in proper position   **Fig. 43.** Left hand with collapsed knuckles

Note that the long joint will rest into the left hand near the base of the index finger. Some bassoonists put some material (moleskin, cork, leather, etc.) on this part of the long joint to cushion their hand and/or facilitate a more advantageous hand position.

The "home position" of the left thumb is on the whisper key. The fleshy part of the thumb should touch the key and the thumb should extend horizontally from there (Fig. 44).

On some notes the first finger of the left hand will cover only a portion of the tone hole, a technique known as "half-hole." To find and control proper half-hole position, the finger should roll – not slide – slightly downward (Fig 45). The amount of half-hole, i.e., the amount of the hole that should remain covered, will very slightly depending upon the note being played.

Fig. 44. LH thumb in playing position   **Fig. 45.** LH1 in half-hole position

Left thumb in the low register

The notes of the lowest register are fingered to a large extent by the left thumb. The proper use of the thumb in this register requires special explanation.

The Low E key (a.k.a. "pancake key") also closes the whisper key automatically. (One should always check this connection before playing to make sure that it is working properly; see "Assembly," p. 18.) This allows the whisper key to remain closed while the left thumb manipulates the four thumb keys for the low register.

For Low D and Low E♭, the Low D key must be depressed. There are essentially three positions that the thumb may be in while depressing this key. In the first, the thumb is also on the whisper key. To do this, simply keep your thumb on the whisper key and lower the second knuckle so that it depresses the Low D key (Fig. 46). Note that here the key contacts the thumb near the second knuckle. The second position is very similar, but the thumb lifts off the whisper key (Fig. 47). In the third position, the thumb is closer to the Low C key. To do this, first put your thumb in the second position. Contacting the key with the middle of your thumb on the outside edge of the key, slide the thumb down towards the Low C key (Fig. 48). The long narrow shape of the Low D key is designed to allow you to move between these three positions easily. Which position the thumb should be in depends on the notes directly before and after the Low D or Low E♭. Strive to use these three positions to your advantage by always having your thumb ready for the next note.

Fig. 46. Low D, position 1

Fig. 47. Low D, position 2

Fig. 48. Low D, position 3

To depress the Low C key, continue sliding your thumb along the Low D key until it contacts the Low C key. Note that you should still contact the key on its outside edge with the middle of your thumb (Fig. 49). Also note that the Low C key automatically closes the Low D key. To depress the Low B and B♭ keys, simply lower the top portion of the thumb (Figs. 50 and 51). Note that the Low B key depresses the Low C key (and also the Low D key) automatically. (Make sure that the connections between these keys remains in proper adjustment!) Also note that the Low B♭ key works independently, i.e., it does not close the other keys also. Hence, to finger Low B♭ one must depress both the Low B and Low B♭ keys fully.

Fig. 49. LH thumb, Low C

Fig. 50. LH thumb, Low B

Fig. 51. LH thumb, Low B♭

Right hand

The "home position" of the right hand will have the index finger over the first tone hole on the boot; the middle finger over the second tone hole. The ring finger and pinky will be directly over and may even lightly touch the G key and Low F key respectively (Figs. 52 and 53). The use of a handrest (crutch) will be addressed below.

Fig. 52. RH in "home position" with crutch   **Fig. 53.** RH without crutch

The thumb should be positioned directly over the Low E key, and may touch it lightly or rest on the guard near it (Fig. 54). Avoid resting the thumb against the body of the instrument above the Bb key (Fig. 55).

Fig. 54. RH thumb, proper position   **Fig. 55.** RH thumb, improper position

Use of a handrest/crutch is optional. (Compare Figures 52 and 53 above.) There are many fine players who play with a crutch, and also many fine players who play without one. Some bassoonists have a custom-made crutch or other mechanism for positioning their right hand. I recommend the use of a crutch (unless one's hands are not large enough) for two reasons: it helps to steady the bassoon, especially when playing "whisper key F" which has no fingers down; and it promotes a more ergonomic position for the right hand with the fingers closer to their neutral position. This facilitates technique and reduces the risk of medical issues.

Drop your right hand to your side and allow it to relax completely. It will naturally
assume its neutral position (Fig. 56). Note the slight curvature to the fingers and the
space between the index finger and thumb. The right hand can stay rather close to this
position in performance; one needs only to spread the fingers slightly to get them in
playing position. When your hand is in playing position, you'll notice a gap between the
side of the boot joint and your hand (just between the thumb and index finger.) The
crutch fills this gap and allows a contact point to steady the right hand while maintaining
this position.

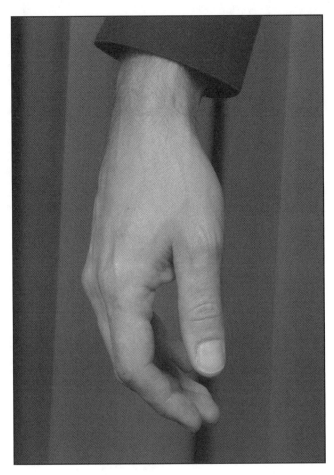

Fig. 56. RH in neutral position

Selected Bibliography

This bibliography is by design quite short and is intended to direct bassoonists to quality, important sources of further information.

Music Reference

Randel, Don Michael, ed. *The Harvard Concise Dictionary of Music and Musicians.* Cambridge, MA: Belknap Press, 1999.

Sadie, S. and J. Tyrrell, eds. *The New Grove Dictionary of Music and Musicians.* London: Macmillan, 2001.

Bassoon (General/Multi-Topic)

Apfelstadt, Marc and Ronald Klimko. *Bassoon Performance Practice, Teaching Materials, Techniques and Methods.* Moscow, ID: School of Music Publications, University of Idaho, 1993.

Popkin, Mark and Loren Glickman. *Bassoon Reed Making including Bassoon Repair, Maintenance and Adjustment, and an Approach to Bassoon Playing,* rev. ed. Northfield, IL: Instrumentalist Co., 1987.

Seltmann, Werner and Günter Angerhöfer [translations by William Waterhouse]. *Fagott-Schule: in Sechs Bänden [Bassoon Tutor: in Six Volumes].* Mainz; New York: Schott, 1977–1984.

Vonk, Maarten, trans. by Bruce Gordon. *A Bundle of Joy: A Practical Handbook for the Bassoon.* Amersfoort: FagotAtelier Maarten Vonk, 2007.

Waterhouse, William. *Bassoon.* London: Kahn & Averill, 2003.

In addition to the above books, the International Double Reed Society provides valuable in-print and online resources to its members and to the double reed community in general, and also hosts conferences and competitions. Learn more at www.idrs.org.

History of the Bassoon

Joppig, Gunther, trans. by Alfred Clayton. *The Oboe and the Bassoon.* Portland, OR: Amadeus, 1988.

Kopp, James B. *The Bassoon.* New Haven: Yale University Press, 2012.

Waterhouse, William. "Bassoon." *The New Grove Dictionary of Music and Musicians,* ed. S. Sadie and J. Tyrrell. London: Macmillan, 2001, vol. 2, pp. 873–895.

Bassoon Repertoire

Bulling, Burchard. *Fagott Bibliographie.* Wilhelmshaven: Florian Noetzel Verlag; Heinrichshofen Bücher, 1989.

Koenigsbeck, Bodo. *Bassoon Bibliography.* Monteux, FR: Musica Rara, 1994.

Performance

Cooper, Lewis Hugh and Howard Toplansky. *Essentials of Bassoon Technique (German System).* Union, NJ: H. Toplansky, 1968.

McGill, David. *Sound in Motion: A Performer's Guide to Greater Musical Expression.* Bloomington, IN: Indiana University Press, 2007.

Weait, Christopher. *Bassoon Strategies for the Next Level.* Worthington, OH: Christopher Weait, LLC, 2003.

Weisberg, Arthur. *The Art of Wind Playing.* Galesville, MD: Meredith Music Publications, 2007.

Ornamentation/Performance Practice

Brown, Clive. *Classical and Romantic Performing Practice 1750–1900*. Oxford; New York: Oxford University Press, 1999.

Brown, Howard Mayer and Stanley Sadie, eds. *Performance Practice, Vol. 2: Music after 1600*. New York: W. W. Norton, 1990.

Donington, Robert. *Baroque Music, Style and Performance: a Handbook*, 1st American ed. New York: Norton, 1982.

_____ . *The Interpretation of Early Music*, new rev. ed. New York: Norton, 1989.

Neumann, Frederick. *Ornamentation and Improvisation in Mozart*. Princeton, NJ: Princeton University Press, 1986.

_____ . *Performance Practice of the Seventeenth and Eighteenth Centuries*. New York: Schirmer Books, 1993.

Quantz, Johann Joachim, translation, notes, and introduction by Edward R. Reilly. *On Playing the Flute*, 2nd ed. New York: Schirmer Books, 1985.

Reeds

Weait, Christopher. *Bassoon Reed-Making: An Illustrated Basic Method*. Worthington, OH: Christopher Weait, 2008.

Weait, Christopher. *Improve Your Bassoon Reed*. Kawartha Lakes, Ont: KIVU Studios, a division of KIVU Nature Inc., 2008. DVD.

Works Cited

Cooper, Lewis Hugh and Howard Toplansky. *Essentials of Bassoon Technique (German System)*. Union, NJ: H. Toplansky, 1968.

Hodges, Woodrow Joe. "A Biographical Dictionary of Bassoonists Born before 1825." Ph.D. dissertation, University of Iowa, 1980.

Polonchak, Richard M. *Primary Handbook for Bassoon*. Meredith Music Publications, 1982.

Solow, Jeffrey. "A Who's Who for Cellists." *Strings Magazine* 16:4:98 (Nov.–Dec. 2001), pp. 80–87.

Spaniol, Douglas E. "The History of the Weissenborn Method for Bassoon." *Celebrating Double Reeds*, ed. T. Ewell. Baltimore: International Double Reed Society, 2009.

Waterhouse, William. "Bassoon." *The New Grove Dictionary of Music and Musicians*, ed. S. Sadie and J. Tyrrell. London: Macmillan, 2001, vol. 2, pp. 873–895.

_____. Preface to *Bassoon Studies, Op.8, No. 2 for Advanced Pupils*. Vienna: Universal Editions, 1987

_____. "New Light on the Weissenborn Family." *The Double Reed*, Vol. 30, No. 2, 2007, pp. 35–44.

_____. Liner notes for *Romanze of Weissenborn*. Equilibrium EQ 72, 2004.

Weait, Christopher. *Bassoon Reed-Making: An Illustrated Basic Method*. Worthington, OH: Christopher Weait, LLC, 2008.

Weissenborn, Julius. *Practical Bassoon-School with Complete Theoretical Explanations for Teacher and Pupil*. Leipzig: R. Forberg, 1887.

_____ . *Practical Bassoon-School with Complete Theoretical Explanations for Teacher and Pupil*. 7th ed., ed. Carl Schaefer. Leipzig: Rob. Forberg, 1903 (preface 1920).

_____ . *Method for Bassoon*, ed. Fred Bettoney. Boston: Cundy-Bettoney Co., 1930.

_____ . *Practical Method for the Bassoon*, ed. W.F. Ambrosio. New York: Carl Fischer, 1941.

_____ . *Method for Bassoon*, ed. Fred Bettoney. Boston: Cundy-Bettoney Co., 1950.

PRACTICAL EXERCISES

I

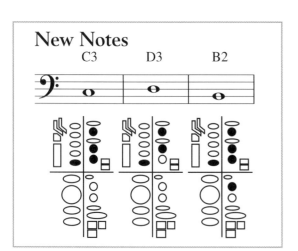

New Notes

C3　　　D3　　　B2

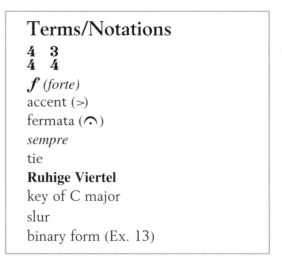

Terms/Notations

$\frac{4}{4}$　$\frac{3}{4}$

f (forte)

accent (>)

fermata (⌢)

sempre

tie

Ruhige Viertel

key of C major

slur

binary form (Ex. 13)

Play Exercise 1 on the reed and bocal only. Strive for a full, strong tone with clean beginnings and ends of notes (think "tah" or "toh"). Pitch should be approximately C4 (middle C) as shown. Play with "standard" articulation the first time, accented (>) articulation on the repeats.

For Exercises 2–14, always play with a full tone and dynamic (*f sempre*) and hold all notes for their full duration. All exercises are "Ruhige Viertel" (calmly, quarter note gets the beat).

52

II

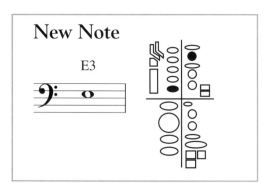

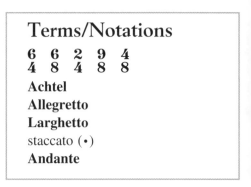

For all exercises, play with a full tone and dynamic (*f sempre*) and hold all notes for their full duration unless otherwise marked.

8. **Ruhige Achtel (in 6)**

9. **Allegretto**

10. **Larghetto (in 9)**

11. **Ruhige Viertel**   D.E.S.

12. **Ruhige Achtel (in 4)***   C.J.W./D.E.S.

*originally notated in ²⁄₄ time

13. **Andante**

Student

Teacher

54

III

IV

New Note

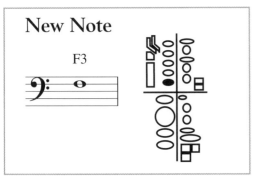

F3

Terms/Notations

"wedge" or strong staccato (▾)
Moderato
Sostenuto
Alla breve
¢ (2/2)
breath mark (,)

The wedge (▾) indicates a strong staccato. That is, the note should be played short, separated, and accented. There are several other ways to indicate this type of articulation. The notations below are performed in essentially the same fashion:

1. **Moderato**

f sempre

9

2. **Sostenuto**

3. **Moderato**

4. **Allegretto**

5. **Alla breve**

6. **Allegretto**

7. **L'istesso tempo**

57

8. Moderato

9. L'istesso tempo

10. Moderato

Bassoonists must learn to find appropriate points in the music to breathe (inhale). Ideally this is done at rests. When this is not possible, breaths should be taken at the ends of phrases or at other logical, natural pausing points in the music. Sometimes breaths are indicated by a comma (,). Almost always, the note *before* the breath is shortened slightly so that the next note may begin on time. [Some people also use this mark (∨) to indicate a breathing point. Sometimes the comma means to breathe and/or delay the next note slightly, i.e., take a slight pause, as in speaking.]

11. Andante

V

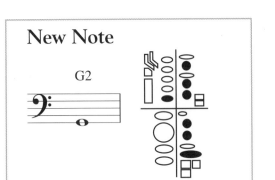

New Note

G2

Terms/Notations

Mässiges Walzertempo
Allegro moderato
Meno allegro
Più lento
Fine
Da capo sin' al fine
rounded binary form (Ex. 10)

1. Andante

2. Moderato

3. Allegretto

4. L'istesso tempo

5. Moderato

59

VI

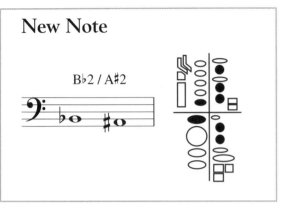

New Note

Bb2 / A#2

Terms/Notations

Lento
key signature
3
2
common time (**C**)
key of D minor
Adagio di molto
key of F major
ritardando (ritard. or *rit.)*
a tempo

What is the difference between **6/4** and **3/2** ?

VII

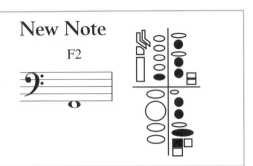

New Note

F2

Terms/Notations

F major scale

$\frac{4}{2}$ $\frac{3}{8}$

modulation

Minuetto

Patetico

1. Moderato

C.J.W./D.E.S.

f sempre

2. Moderato F Major Scale. Also see Supplement Exercises 1—10 and 35—36.

C.J.W./D.E.S.

3. Moderato

4. Andante

5. Andante

6. Andantino

7. Minuetto *In sehr mässigem Tempo* (In a very moderate tempo)

8. Patetico *Scharf akzentuiert* (Sharply accented)

64

VIII

New Note

A♭2 / G♯2

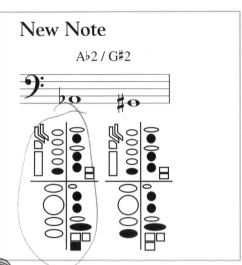

A♭2/G♯2 has two fingerings. The first one shown ("pinky G♯2") is the more commonly used fingering. The second fingering ("thumb G♯2") is used rather sparingly, usually when the note is preceded or followed directly by "pinky F♯" (introduced in XII.a).

Terms/Notations

Ruhig
sempre staccato (stacc.)
Molto
p (piano)
mp (mezzo piano)
mf (mezzo forte)
< *(crescendo)*
> *(decrescendo)*

*A2 in original.

IX

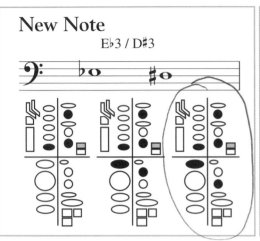

New Note
Eb3 / D#3

The first fingering is the basis for all three and the simplest to use technically, but it may be unstable. The second fingering is more stable, lower in pitch, and quiet. The third is stable, sharper and brighter in tone. Note that for all three fingerings use of the "resonance key" (Low Eb key) is optional. (The resonance key is added to many fingerings to improve tone and/or pitch.)

Terms/Notations

portato (˙˙˙˙˙ ‿ ˙˙˙˙˙)
key of C minor
con espressione
ritenuto (riten.)
ternary form (Ex. 6)
change of mode (major/minor)
dolce

X

New Note

C♯3 / D♭3

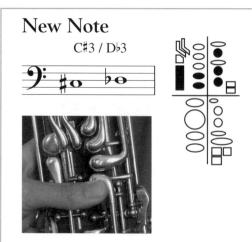

Note that in playing C♯3/D♭3, the left thumb depresses three keys (the whisper key, the C♯ key, and the Low D key). Also note that the thumb contacts only the lower part of the C♯ key. To do this, "roll" the thumb up to the C♯ key. Do not lift the thumb up off the whisper key and then put it back down.

Terms/Notations

key of A major

key of A♭ major

key/scale of F minor

mfp

Marcia funebre

diminuendo (dim. or dimin.)

1. **Slowly** D.E.S.

f

This passage is a good test for your reed. If the C♯'s and/or E's are flat, the reed is likely too long and/or soft.

2. **Slowly** D.E.S.

f

3. **Andante** C.J.W./D.E.S.

mf

4. **Andante** C.J.W./D.E.S.

mf

(Also see Supplement Exercises 1–10 and 35-37.)

70

XI

New Note

G3

G3 is the first upper register note to be introduced in this book. The use of the "half-hole" (LH1) helps this note to speak in the upper octave, much like an octave key on other woodwind instruments. To open the half-hole, roll the finger downward. Do not slide it, nor lift it and set it back down. The size of the half-hole opening is critical in getting the note to speak.

Terms/Notations

half-hole
key of B♭ major
Andante con moto
marcato
Allegro non tanto
mit vollem Ton
Allegro vivace
rf
Canon
un poco rallentando

72

XII.a

New Notes

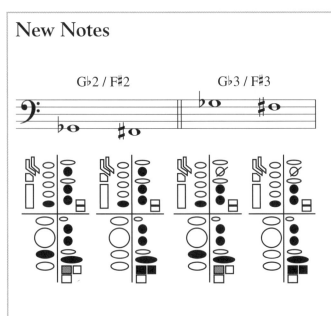

Gb2 / F#2   Gb3 / F#3

Gb/F# in the lower octave has two fingerings. The first one shown ("thumb F#") is the more commonly used fingering. Note that when the thumb F# key is depressed, the Low F key automatically closes. The second fingering ("pinky F#") is used primarily to avoid a "jump" for the left thumb, such as when F# is preceded or followed directly by Bb. The upper octave has the same two fingerings as the lower octave, but with half-hole on LH1. The half-hole for F#3 should be slightly more open than for G3 so that the F#3 speaks cleanly (see photo).

Terms/Notations

chromatic scale (also see Supplement Exercises 32–34)

assai

Canzonetta

4. **Andante con moto** C.J.W. Op. 8, No. 1/D.E.S.

(Also see Supplement Exercise 32.)

5. **Andantino** (Canzonetta)

XII.b

New Note

A3

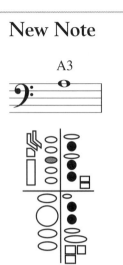

A3 is the first note to be introduced that has a fingering with the whisper key open (not depressed). The open whisper key acts as a vent to help A3 speak in the upper octave (like the half-hole on G3 and F♯3). Often, however, the whisper key alone does not provide enough of a vent for A3 to be played cleanly, so one must also use the High A key as a "speaker" key. One option is to press the High A key for the duration of the note, but doing so can result in an out-of-tune and/or unstable tone. As a result, bassoonists often "flick" this key by touching it quickly at the beginning of the note rather than holding it down; this is enough to create the necessary "vent." It is especially important to use the High A key when A3 is: 1) approached by a slur going over the break (from F3 and below); 2) approached by a slur from certain higher notes, like F4 (to be introduced later); or 3) tongued. The use of the High A key is less crucial when A3 is approached by a slur from a small interval, like from F♯3 or G3. In this book, notes that require the speaker key are marked with this symbol [∘], as was done in Weissenborn's original edition.

Terms/Notations

speaker keys (also known as flick or vent keys)
key/scale of G minor
key/scale of G major
Allegro ma non troppo
rallentando (rall.)
con energico

XIII

New Notes

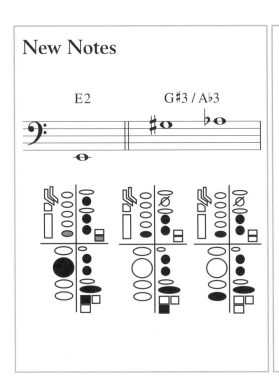

E2   G#3 / A♭3

Closing the Low E key (also known as the "pancake key") also closes the whisper key. Hence, your left thumb can be on or off the whisper key when playing E2. Unless there is good reason to lift it, it is best to leave your thumb on the whisper key. Adding the Low C# key helps prevent E2 from being sharp in pitch and improves the tone quality.

G#3 has the same two fingerings as the lower octave, but with a half-hole on LH1. The half-hole for G#3 should be slightly less open than for G3 so that the G#3 speaks cleanly (see photo.)

Terms/Notations

A minor scale
Moderato assai
fz (forzando)
A major scale
key/scale of E minor
key/scale of E major
key/scale of F# minor
key/scale of F# major
breve (double whole note) |O|
Alla marcia
✕ (double sharp)

1. Slowly   D.E.S.

2. Slowly A Natural Minor Scale. Also practice the harmonic and melodic forms.   C.J.W./D.E.S.

(Also see Supplement Exercises 1–10, 32, and 35-37.)

3. Moderato assai

4. Moderato

5. **Slowly** A Major Scale. Also see Supplement Exercises 1—10, 32, and 35—37.

C.J.W./D.E.S.

6. **Moderato**

7. **Slowly** E Natural Minor Scale. Also practice the harmonic and melodic forms.

C.J.W./D.E.S.

(Also see Supplement Exercises 1–10, 32, and 35-37.)

8. **Moderato**

C.J.W./D.E.S.

mit vollem Ton, marcato

9. **Andante**

C.J.W./D.E.S.

10. **Slowly** E Major Scale. Also see Supplement Exercises 1—10, and 35—37.

C.J.W./D.E.S.

11. **Andante**

C.J.W./D.E.S.

XIV

New Notes

A#3 / B♭3   D2

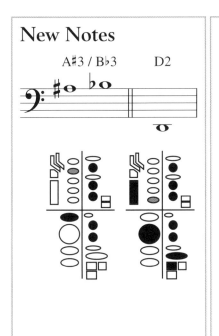

Terms/Notations

B♭ major scale
key/scale of B♭ minor
D minor scale
key/scale of D major

Like A3, B♭3 is vented by lifting the whisper key, and also needs additional venting most of the time. Most bassoonists use the High C key for this (as shown in the above diagram), although some prefer the High A key. Here too, one may hold the speaker key down for the duration of the note, or one may flick the key at the beginning of the note. (B♭3 is usually rather stable and well in-tune when holding down the High C key.) As with A3, it is especially important to flick or vent B♭3 when it is: 1) approached from a slur going over the break (from F3 and below); 2) approached by a slur from certain higher notes, like F4 (which will be introduced later); or 3) tongued. The use of a speaker key on B♭3 is less crucial when it is approached by a slur from a small interval. In this book, notes that require the speaker key are marked with this symbol [∘].

For now, when playing D2, keep your left thumb on the whisper key and flatten the lower part of the thumb to depress the Low D key. The Low D key will be contacted by the middle of the thumb (see p. 44, Fig. 46). Playing Low D without the thumb on the whisper key will be discussed later.

82

*This and other duets marked "C.J.W./D.E.S." were originally single-voice etudes. The second bassoon parts were added by this author.

84

XV

New Notes

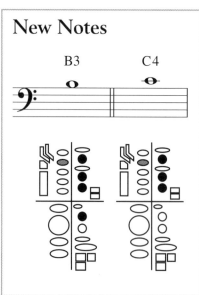

As with A3 and B♭3, B3 and C4 are vented by lifting the whisper key, and also need additional venting most of the time. The High C key should be used as the vent key for both of these notes. Here too, one may hold the speaker key down for the duration of the note, or one may flick the key at the beginning of the note. (Both of these notes are usually rather stable and well in-tune when holding down the High C key.) It is especially important to flick or vent B3 and C4 when they are: 1) approached from a slur going over the break (from F3 and below); 2) approached by a slur from certain higher notes, like F♯4 (which will be introduced later); and 3) tongued. The use of a speaker key on B3 and C4 is less crucial when they are approached by a slur from a small interval. In this book, notes that require the speaker key are marked with this symbol [∘].

Terms/Notations

sonoro
C major scale
C minor scale
dolcissimo
key/scale of B minor
key/scale of B major
key/scale of G♯ minor

4. Moderato

5. Andantino

dolce

6. Slowly C Major Scale. Also see Supplement Exercises 1—10, 13, 32, and 35—37. C.J.W./D.E.S.

(Also see Supplement Exercises 1–10, 13, 32, and 35-37.)

7. Andante

dolcissimo

8. Slowly C Natural Minor Scale. Also practice the harmonic and melodic forms. C.J.W./D.E.S.

(Also see Supplement Exercises 1–10, 13, and 35-37.)

9. Andante

dolcissimo

10. **Slowly** B Natural Minor Scale. Also practice the harmonic and melodic forms.

(Also see Supplement Exercises 1–10, 13, 32, and 35-37.)

11. **Allegro**

12. **Slowly** B Major Scale. Also see Supplement Exercises 1—10, 13, and 35—37.

(Also see Supplement Exercises 1–12, 32, and 35-37.)

13. **Allegro**

14. **Slowly** G♯ Natural Minor Scale. Also practice the harmonic and melodic forms.

15. **Andante***

C.J.W./D.E.S.

Student

Teacher

cresc.

cresc.

*This exercise was originally in G Major. In addition to adding the second bassoon part, this author has changed the key to G♯ minor and altered the first bassoon part.

XVI.a

New Note

Eb2 / D#2

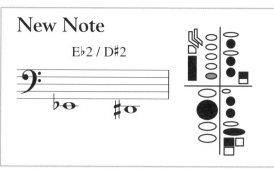

As with E2 and D2, the whisper key is optional on Eb2 (it will be closed automatically by the Low E key). For now, it's best to keep your thumb on the whisper key and depress the Low D key as discussed in Lesson XIV.

Terms/Notations

key/scale of Eb major

Langsam

1. Andante

2. Slowly Eb Major Scale. Also see Supplement Exercises 1—12, 14—16, 32, and 35—37.

C.J.W./D.E.S.

3. Alla breve

Student

mit vollem Ton
Teacher

4. Andante

mit vollem Ton

88

XVI.b

New Note

C♯4 / D♭4

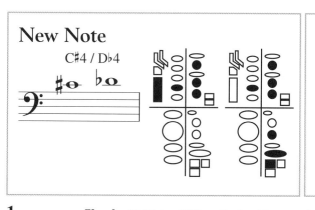

There are two basic fingerings for C♯4; the "short" fingering (first one shown) and the "long" fingering (second one shown). The short fingering tends to be a little darker and lower in pitch; the long fingering tends to be brighter and higher in pitch. No speaker key is needed for this note.

Terms/Notations

key/scale of E♭ minor
Maestoso
key/scale of C♯ minor
poco
key/scale of D♭ major
A♭ major scale

1. **Slowly** E♭ Natural Minor Scale. Also practice the harmonic and melodic forms.　　　　C.J.W./D.E.S.

(Also see Supplement Exercises 1–12, 14–16, and 35-37.)

2. **Alla breve**
Student
mit vollem Ton
Teacher

3. **Andante maestoso**　　　　C.J.W. Op. 8, No. 1/D.E.S.
f marcato

4. **Slowly** C♯ Natural Minor Scale. Also practice the harmonic and melodic forms.　　　　C.J.W./D.E.S.

(Also see Supplement Exercises 1–10, 13, 32, and 35-37.)

XVII

New Note

C2

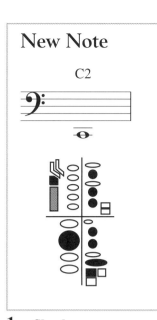

To find the proper thumb position for C2 ("Low C"), begin by fingering D2 ("Low D") with your left thumb on both the Low D key and the whisper key. Take the tip of your thumb off the whisper key, but leave the middle of the thumb on the Low D Key. Next, slide your thumb down the left edge of the Low D key until it contacts the Low C key. This is the proper thumb position for fingering Low C. Note that the middle part of the thumb contacts the left edge of the Low C key. Also note that the Low C key automatically closes the Low D key; there is no need to hold down both keys. Also note that the whisper key will remain closed because the Low E key is depressed (see "Left thumb in the low register," pp. 43–44, for photos and additional information). When approaching C2 from D2 or E♭2, the thumb should move as described above. When approaching C2 from E2, keep your thumb off the whisper key for E2; instead, keep it close to the Low C key. When approaching C2 from F2 or above, the thumb must "jump" from the whisper key to the Low C key.

Terms/Notations

Risoluto

interval

octave

third

fourth

fifth

caesura (///)

92

94

XVIII.a

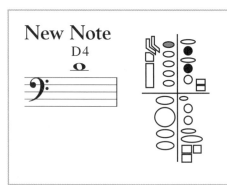

New Note
D4

In most cases, the whisper key alone will provide adequate venting for D4. It may need additional venting when slurring to it over the break (from F3 and below); in these cases, it's best to vent D4 by flicking the High D key. If your bassoon does not have a High D key, flick the High C key very quickly and lightly, or simply vent D4 with the whisper key alone.

Terms/Notations

espressivo (espress.)

Trio

compound ternary form (Ex. 6)

4. **Slowly** D Major Scale (2 Octaves). Also see Supplement Exercises 17—31, 33, 38—47, and 62—64.

C.J.W./D.E.S.

5. **Moderato**

C.J.W. Op. 8, No. 1/D.E.S.

Fine

D.C. sin al Fine

6. **Allegretto**

C.J.W./D.E.S.

XVIII.b

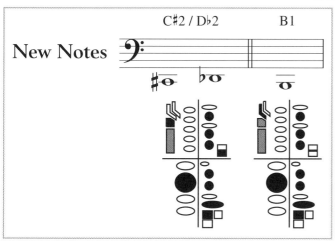

When fingering C♯2, the left thumb should be in the same position as when fingering C2 (see Lesson XVII).

See p. 44 for information and a photo of left thumb position when playing B1. Note that the Low B key automatically depresses the Low C and Low D keys. (Check the alignment of these keys.)

Terms/Notations

fp (fortepiano)

sf (sforzando)

98

5. **L'istesso tempo**

C.J.W./D.E.S.

dolce

6. **Moderato assai**

dolce

f

p

sf

7. **Slowly** B Natural Minor Scale. Also practice the harmonic and melodic forms.

C.J.W./D.E.S.

f

(Also see Supplement Exercises 17–31, 33, 38–47, and 62–64.)

8. **Andante**

C.J.W./D.E.S.

Student

dolce

Teacher

dolce

fz

fz

XIX

New Notes

Bb1 is the lowest note on most bassoons. To finger Bb1 ("Low Bb"), begin by fingering B1 as described in the previous lesson. Keeping the Low B key depressed, lower the tip of the thumb until it depresses the Low Bb key also. Note that the Bb key works independently; that is, it doesn't close any other keys. Hence, you need to be sure to keep both the Low B and Low Bb keys fully closed (see p. 44).

When fingering Eb4, the first finger of the right hand is optional. Lifting it will help the note speak on many slurs; closing it will make some technical passages easier. There is almost no difference in tone and pitch between the two fingerings.

100

9. L'istesso tempo

10. **Slowly** B♭ Natural Minor Scale. Also practice the harmonic and melodic forms.

C.J.W./D.E.S.

(Also see Supplement Exercises 17–31, and 38–47.)

11. **Moderato**

New Notes

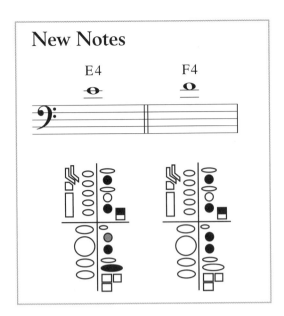

As is the case with E♭4, the first finger of the right hand is optional when playing E4. Lifting it will help the note speak on many slurs; closing it will make some technical passages easier. There is almost no difference in tone and pitch between the two fingerings.

(Also see Supplement Exercises 17–31, 33, 38–55, and 59–64.)

104

XXI.a

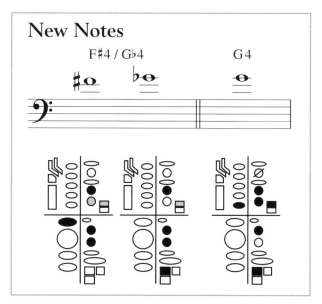

New Notes

F♯4 / G♭4   G4

There are many ways to finger F♯4; the two most common are shown. With the first fingering, LH3 should be lifted to help slurs speak and lowered when tonguing the note. With both fingerings, use of the resonance key is optional.

Notice that G4 has half-hole for LH1. As is the case with all half-hole notes, the whisper key should be closed and the size of the half-hole set so that the note speaks well.

1. Slowly   D.E.S.

2. (Slowly)

mit vollem Ton

3. Slowly G Major Scale. Also see Supplement Exercises 17—31, 33, 38—47, 48—58, 62.

C.J.W./D.E.S.

4. Andante

Student

Teacher

5. Allegro

6. Slowly G Natural Minor Scale. Also pracrtice the harmonic and melodic forms.

C.J.W./D.E.S.

(Also see Supplement Exercises 17–31, 38–47, 59–61, and 63–64.)

7. Marcia

poco *f* risoluto

XXI.b

1. **Slowly** E♭ Major Scale. Also see Supplement Exercises 17—31, 33, 38—45, 56—68, and 62.

C.J.W./D.E.S.

2. **Slowly**

mit vollem Ton

3. **Energico**

poco f

4. **Slowly** C Natural Minor Scale. Also practice the harmonic and melodic forms.

(Also see Supplement Exercises 17–31, 38–47, 59–61, and 63–64.)

5. **Mässig schnell** (Moderately fast)

C.J.W. Op. 8, No. 1/D.E.S.

6. **Andante**

7. **Langsam**

Student

dolce

Teacher

cantabile

XXII

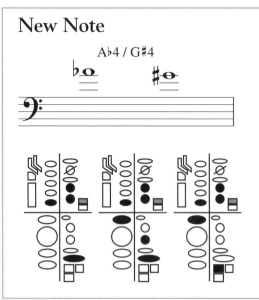

New Note

A♭4 / G♯4

Terms/Notations

Sehr ruhiges Zeitmass

It can be difficult to get A♭4 to speak cleanly. Listen carefully to the beginning of the note—if the note "cracks," adjust the size of the half-hole opening (it will probably need to be quite small). Be sure to have the whisper key closed whenever possible.

Any of the three fingerings given can be used as a standard fingering for this note. The first is perhaps the most common. The second is flatter in pitch and fuller in tone; the third can help alleviate fingering difficulties in this register.

1. Slowly — D.E.S.

2. Slowly A♭ Major Scale. Also see Supplement Exercises 17—31, 33, 38—58, and 62. — C.J.W./D.E.S.

3. Langsam — C.J.W./D.E.S.

C.J.W./D.E.S.

112

6. **Moderato**

mit vollem Ton

7. **Moderato**

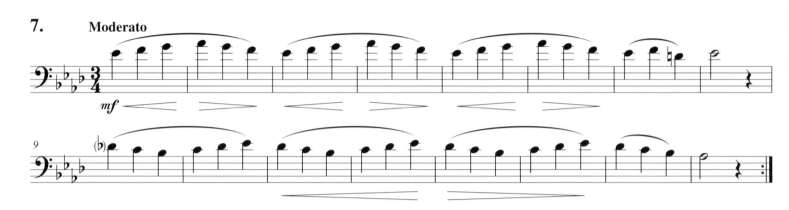

8. **Slowly** F Natural Minor Scale. Also practice the harmonic and melodic forms.

C.J.W./D.E.S.

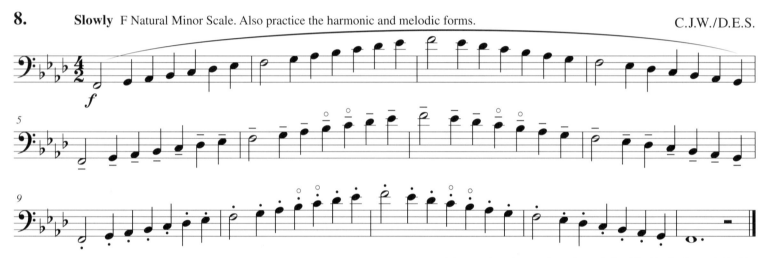

(Also see Supplement Exercises 17–31, 38–47, 59–61, and 63–64.)

9. **Ruhiges Zeitmass**

10. **Slowly** D♭ Major Scale. Also see Supplement Exercises 17—31, 33, 38—58, and 62. C.J.W./D.E.S.

11. **Sehr ruhiges Zeitmass**

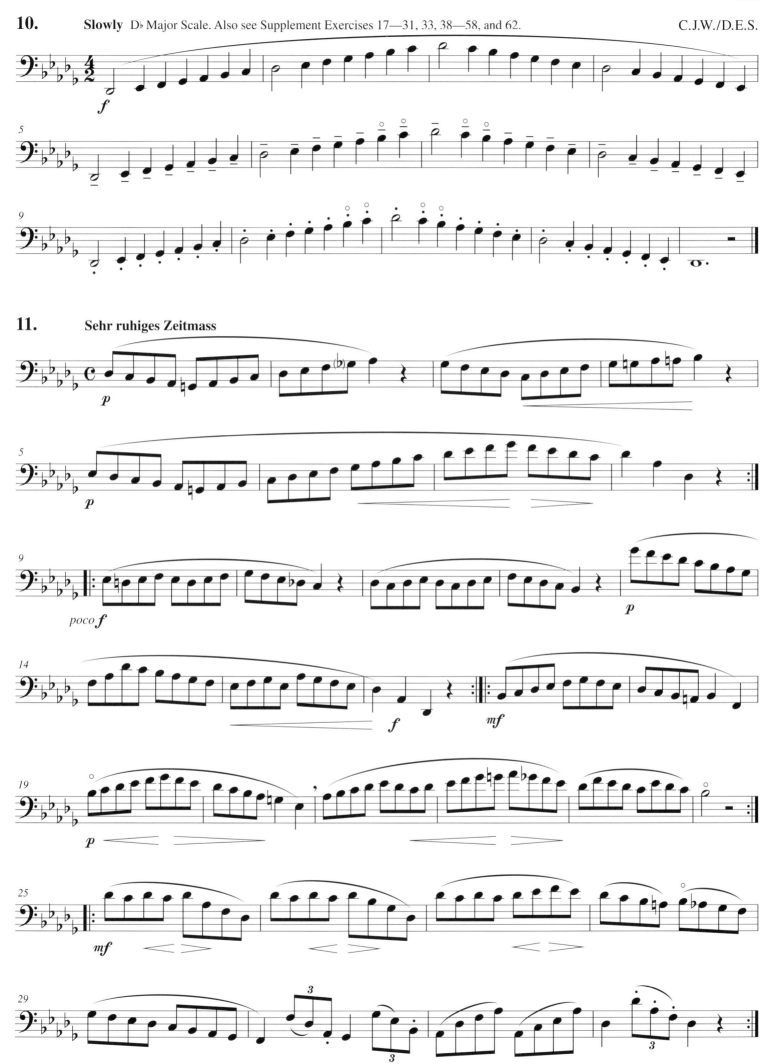

XXIII.a

New Note

A4

As is the case with A♭4, there are three "standard" fingerings for A4. Note that the right hand for each of the three choices is identical to that of A♭4, and their usage is also the same: the first is perhaps the most common; the second is flatter in pitch and fuller in tone; the third can help alleviate fingering difficulties in this register. One should use the same right hand combination for both A♭4 and A4. Also note that the left thumb must depress both the C♯ key and the High A key.

1. Slowly A Natural Minor Scale. Also practice the harmonic and melodic forms.

C.J.W./D.E.S.

(Also see Supplement Exercises 17–31, 33, 38–55, 59–61, and 63.)

C.J.W./D.E.S.

2. Langsam

mit vollem Ton

3. Allegro moderato

dolce

4. **Slowly** A Major Scale. Also see Supplement Exercises 17—31, 38—47, 56—58, 62, and 64.

C.J.W./D.E.S.

5. **Andante con moto**

6. **Slowly** F♯ Natural Minor Scale. Also practice the harmonic and melodic forms.
C.J.W./D.E.S.

(Also see Supplement Exercises 17–31, 33, 38–55, 59–61, and 63.)

7. **Langsam**
C.J.W./D.E.S.

XXIII.b

Terms/Notations
giusto

1. **Slowly** E Major Scale. Also see Supplement Exercises 17—31, 38—58, 62, and 64.

C.J.W./D.E.S.

2. **Langsam**

mit vollem Ton

3. **Allegro giusto**

to be played:

4. **Slowly** C♯ Natural Minor Scale. Also practice the harmonic and melodic forms.   C.J.W./D.E.S.

(Also see Supplement Exercises 17–31, 33, 38–55, 59–61, and 63–64.)

5. **Andante con moto**

Student

C.J.W./D.E.S.

Teacher

XXIV.a

1. **Slowly**

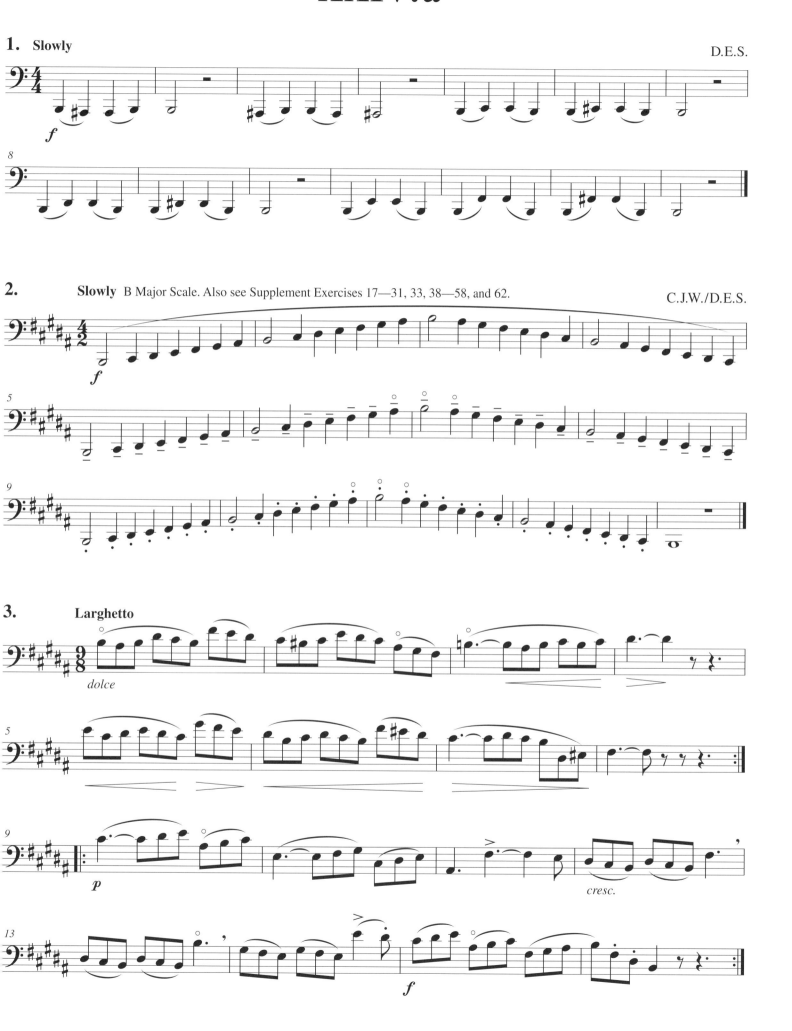

4. **Slowly** G♯ Natural Minor Scale. Also practice the harmonic and melodic forms.

C.J.W./D.E.S.

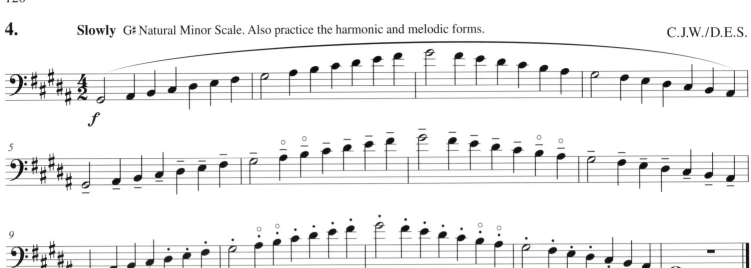

(Also see Supplement Exercises 17–31, 33, 38–55, 59–61, and 63–64.)

C.J.W./D.E.S.

5.

Allegretto

Student

Teacher

XXIV.b

1. **Slowly** F♯ Major Scale. Also see Supplement Exercises 17—31, 33, 38—58 and 62.

C.J.W./D.E.S.

2. **Allegretto**

3. **Slowly** D♯ Natural Minor Scale. Also practice the harmonic and melodic forms.

C.J.W./D.E.S.

(Also see Supplement Exercises 17–31, 33, 38–55, 59–61, and 63–64.)

C.J.W. Op. 8, No. 1/D.E.S.

4. **Andante**

5. **Maestoso** C.J.W./D.E.S.

XXIV.c

Terms/Notations

key/scale of G♭ major

simile (sim.)

Commodo

1. **Slowly** G♭ Major Scale. Also see Supplement Exercises 17—31, 33, 38—58, and 62.

C.J.W./D.E.S.

2. **Allegretto**

3. **Alla marcia**   C.J.W. Op. 8, No. 1/D.E.S.

4. **Slowly** E♭ Natural Minor Scale. Also practice the harmonic and melodic forms.

C.J.W./D.E.S.

(Also see Supplement Exercises 17–31, 33, 38–54, 59–61, and 63–64.)

5. **Commodo**

C.J.W./D.E.S.

Student

Teacher

XXIV.d

Terms/Notations

key/scale of C♯ major

key/scale of A♯ minor

1.   **Slowly**   C♯ Major Scale. Also see Supplement Exercises 17—31, 33, 38—58, and 62.

D.E.S.

C.J.W. Op. 8, No. 1/D.E.S.

2.   **Allegro moderato**

3.   **Slowly**   A♯ Natural Minor Scale. Also practice the harmonic and melodic forms.   D.E.S.

(Also see Supplement Exercises 17–31, 33, 38–54, 59–61, and 63–64.)

4.   **Allegro moderato**   C.J.W. Op. 8, No. 1/D.E.S.

5.   **Andante**   C.J.W. Op. 8, No. 1/D.E.S.

XXIV.e

1. **Slowly** A♭ Natural Minor Scale. Also practice the harmonic and melodic forms.

D.E.S.

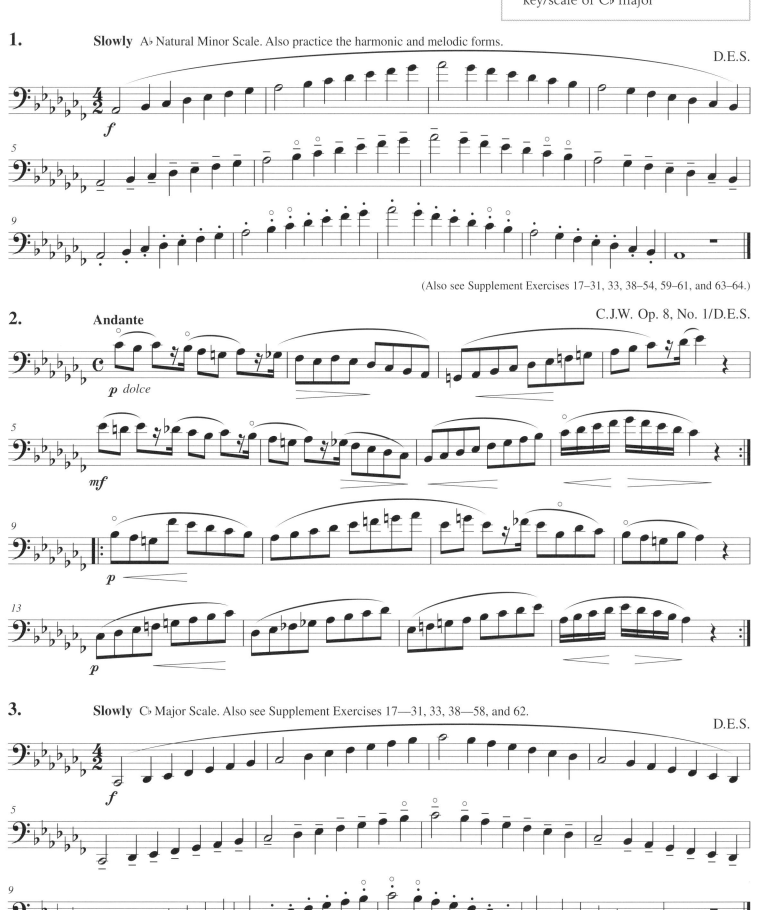

(Also see Supplement Exercises 17–31, 33, 38–54, 59–61, and 63–64.)

2. **Andante**

C.J.W. Op. 8, No. 1/D.E.S.

3. **Slowly** C♭ Major Scale. Also see Supplement Exercises 17—31, 33, 38—58, and 62.

D.E.S.

128

4. Andante*

C.J.W./D.E.S.

*This duet originally appeared at the end of Lesson XXV in the key of C major.

XXV.a

Terms/Notations
tenor clef
rfz (rinforzando)

Music for bassoon is very often written in tenor clef, especially when the range of the music is in the instrument's upper register. Doing so reduces the number of ledger lines, making the music easier to read and write. Bassoonists should become as fluent in reading tenor clef as they are in reading bass clef. Furthermore, students are advised to avoid the common pitfall of becoming fluent in only the upper part of tenor clef. Rather, they should become familiar with the entire range of tenor clef, down to the bottom line of the staff and below.

The figure below illustrates tenor clef notation; in addition, the first exercise is notated in both clefs. Note that the two staves contain identical music – only the clef/notation has changed.

C.J.W. Op. 8, No. 1/D.E.S.

130

XXV.b

New Note

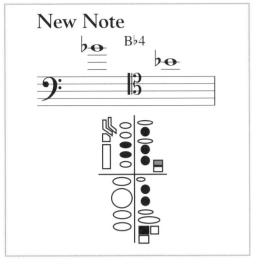

Bb4 is the highest note introduced in this book. Note that the fingering in the left hand is identical to that for A4. If either of these notes do not speak well, adding a High A Key–Whisper Key Bridge to the bassoon may help.

1. Slowly

D.E.S.

C.J.W./D.E.S.

2. Slowly Bb Major Scale (3 Octaves).

(Also see Supplement Exercises 17–31, 34, 38–47, 62, and 64; most of these will need to be extended to three octaves. You may also want to practice the Bb minor scales in a three-octave range.)

3. Moderato

132

4. **Moderato**

dolce

Fine

D.C. al Fine

5. **Poco allegro**

dolce

6. **Andante con moto***

dolce

mf

p

7. **Andante sostenuto***

dolce

*Exercises 6 and 7 originally appeared in the section on tenor clef that followed Lesson XXV. Here they have been incorporated into Lesson XXV.b to give additional practice in reading tenor clef and playing B♭4.

8. **Moderato****

dolce

**This exercise originally appeared in bass clef.

133

9. Moderato assai*

*This exercise originally appeared in bass clef.

10. Andante
C.J.W./D.E.S.

XXVI

Terms/Notations

ornaments (embellishments)	grace note group	turn (∾)
appoggiatura	*Nachschlag*	inverted turn (∾) or (₷)
grace note	mordent (✦)	trill (*tr*) or (*tr*〰〰〰〰)
	inverted mordent (✦)	

Virtually all melodies contain notes that are referred to as "ornaments" or "embellishments"; that is, notes that decorate the main or structural notes of the melody. At times these ornamental notes are written out in full, proper notation and it is quite clear how they should be performed. However, there are also cases in which ornaments are notated with special symbols. In these cases the performance of the ornament is somewhat ambiguous.

Ornaments and their symbols were quite common in music of the Baroque era (ca. 1600–1750) and music of the Classical era (ca.1750–1825). What composers may have intended by each symbol, and how performers may have performed them in each era, are complicated questions whose answers depend upon many factors, including the composer, the instrumentation, the time and place of composition, the specific musical context, etc. Countless pages have been written on this subject by composers, performers, teachers, and scholars. "Performance practice" is a field of musical study that focuses on these and other similar questions. The books on performance practice listed in the bibliography (p. 48) go into much greater detail than there is room for here. The information below is given as an introduction to the most common ornaments that bassoonists encounter today, and is meant to provide information on how to perform these ornaments in a manner that is stylistically reasonable. Please keep in mind that the "rules" presented are, rather, a general guide; virtually all authors and teachers of the subject direct musicians to use good taste and musical judgment in interpreting ornaments.

There are nine ornaments that will be covered in this section: the appoggiatura, the grace note, the grace note group, the *Nachschlag*, the mordent, the inverted mordent, the turn, the inverted turn, and the trill. Each ornament will be introduced with a brief discussion of its possible and most common interpretations. This will be followed by one or more exercises featuring that ornament.

The Appoggiatura

The appoggiatura is perhaps the most common and the most discussed of all the ornaments. The term comes from the Italian verb *"appoggiare,"* meaning, roughly, "to lean (upon)." Hence, an appoggiatura is a note which we lean upon or stress in performance. This is done for two reasons:

- The note is dissonant, meaning it clashes with the bass note or the harmony.
- It falls upon a strong beat (or strong part of the beat) and resolves on a weak beat (or weak part of the beat).

The note of resolution (sometimes referred to as the "main note") is consonant, meaning it does not clash with the bass note or harmony. Appoggiaturas virtually always resolve by a step, either up or down. In fact, appoggiaturas are often notated as regular notes, and one may not even be aware of the fact that a certain note is an appoggiatura (Example 1).

Example 1. Mozart K. 191, mvt. 1, mm. 64–65 (appoggiaturas marked with arrows)

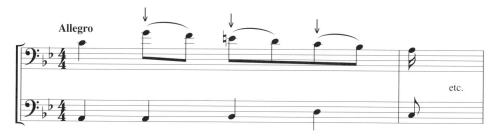

In other cases, appoggiaturas are notated with a smaller-sized note (Example 2). Notice that when the smaller-sized note is used, it is not factored into the meter; the rhythmic values of the main (full-sized) notes alone fill the measure. Appoggiaturas begin where the main note would have begun and their value is subtracted from the main note that follows. (Example 2 and the following examples will help clarify this.)

Example 2. Mozart K. 191, mvt. 1, mm. 64–65 (re-notated with smaller-sized appoggiaturas)

In performance, the appoggiatura is emphasized with dynamic intensity. It resolves to the main note (a consonance) that is then de-emphasized in comparison to the appoggiatura. In other words, one should "lean" on the appoggiatura, and then reduce the intensity and dynamic as it resolves. Appoggiaturas are always slurred to their note of resolution, even if this is not notated. How long should an appoggiatura last? When written as regular notes as in Example 1, the note length is clear; however appoggiaturas should still be leaned upon just like any other. Sometimes the small-note appoggiatura is notated with its true rhythmic value (see Example 3). In such cases the duration of the appoggiatura is also not a question.

Example 3

Practice Exercise 1 on the following page, playing the small-note appoggiaturas according to their written rhythmic values.

Exercise 1

C.J.W./D.E.S.

In some instances, appoggiaturas are notated with a small note that does not accurately reflect the duration of the appoggiatura (this is especially true in earlier Baroque music). These small notes were usually eighth notes, but could be held shorter or (much) longer than an eighth note. In Baroque music two very general rules are:

- If the main note does not have a dot, the appoggiatura is played for half the value of the main note (Example 4A).

- If the main note is dotted, the appoggiatura is played for two-thirds of the value of the main note (Example 4B-C).

Example 4

In Baroque music, it is also possible that appoggiaturas are to be held even longer than shown in Example 4, giving the appoggiatura two-thirds, three-fourths, or even more of the value of the main note (Example 5A). When the main note is followed by a rest, one possible interpretation is to give the appoggiatura the full value of the main note and move the main note over into the rest (see Example 5B-C). Similarly, if the main note is tied, it's possible to give the appoggiatura the value of the first tied note, and give the note of resolution the value of the second tied note (Example 5D).

Example 5

Practice Exercise 2 in two ways. First, apply the general Baroque rule (as in Example 4); then experiment with various other interpretations (as in Example 5).

Exercise 2

Lastly, some consider appoggiaturas to belong to one of two basic categories: the long appoggiatura, which would describe all of the above possible interpretations; and, the short appoggiatura. The short appoggiatura is still a stressed, on-beat dissonance that resolves by a step. The difference is that it is not held as long. The result then becomes something like the figures shown in Example 6A-D.

Example 6

This type of interpretation is a possibility in Baroque music, and may be especially appropriate for the music of Mozart and other classical composers. Play Exercise 3 using short appoggiaturas, both in a triplet rhythm (as in Example 6A-B) and in a sixteenth-note rhythm (as in Example 6C-D).

Exercise 3. Mozart K. 292, mvt. 1, mm. 11–15

The Grace Note

It should be said that the terminology used regarding ornaments can vary quite a bit, and this can lead to a good deal of confusion. This is especially true when discussing appoggiaturas and grace notes. The confusion results largely from the similarity in notation: they are both written with "small notes" that aren't factored into the rhythm of the measure. For the purpose of this book, we shall define the difference between an appoggiatura and a grace note as this: whereas the appoggiatura is played on the beat (or right where the main note would begin if there were no appoggiatura), the grace note is played *just before* the beat (or just before the point where the main note begins). It follows, then, that the grace note takes some time away from the note that precedes it; the appoggiatura takes time from the note that follows it.

Usually the grace note has a slash through the stem, whereas the appoggiatura does not; however, this is not always the case. Hence, a grace note and an appoggiatura (if you accept the above definition of each) may look exactly the same. Furthermore, it is often erroneously said that in Baroque (and even in Classical) music the "small notes" always begin on the beat. While this may be generally true, many sources — both primary and modern — discuss situations where the "small notes" should or could be played before the beat. Nowadays, most performing musicians would say that in music composed after 1825 (or thereabouts) the small notes are all grace notes: that is, from ca. 1825 on, appoggiaturas were written out in regular notation (as in Example 1) instead of with small notes (as in Example 2).

Grace notes that come before the first note of a measure are usually written just after the barline, even though they are played just before the downbeat. Occasionally one sees them written just before the barline.

In performance, grace notes should always be slurred to the main note. In slow tempos they may be somewhat relaxed, but usually they are played very quickly and as close to the beat or main note as possible. This is especially true in faster music or in music that is energetic or militaristic, and when the grace note comes before an accented or staccato main note, as in Exercise 4.

Exercise 4

The Grace Note Group

Sometimes there is more than one grace note leading into a single main note. These usually come in groups of two, three, or four grace notes. They are notated with small sixteenth (or even thirty-second) notes that are all beamed together. Sometimes there is a slash through one corner of the beams, analogous to the slash through the single grace note. All of the performance principles of the single grace note as outlined above pertain to the grace note group. The entire group should be slurred into the main note.

Exercise 5

Exercise 6

The *Nachschlag*

The German term *Vorschlag* is used to denote an appoggiatura and/or grace note. It translates roughly as "pre-beat." The *Nachschlag*, roughly translated as "after-beat," is in some ways the opposite of the *Vorschlag*, but is also similar to the grace note or grace note group in many ways. Like grace notes, it is notated with small notes, usually without a slash. The biggest difference is perhaps conceptual. The *Nachschlag* is seen as the ending to the note it follows, or as a connection or a linking between two notes. (This is clearest when it ends a trill as discussed below.) In practice it is very similar to the grace note/group. Like the grace note, the *Nachschlag* comes just before the next beat or note. Unlike the grace note, the *Nachschlag* is always slurred into from the previous note (Example 7A-D). The note directly after the *Nachschlag* may be tongued (Example 7A) or slurred into (Example 7B-D).

Example 7

Exercise 7

The Mordent

The mordent is found most commonly in Baroque music, but appears in later music as well. The mordent is most typically a quick alternation between the main (written) note and its lower neighbor. Normally the diatonic lower neighbor is used. However, sometimes the lower neighbor is raised to make only a half-step between it and the main note. An accidental may be placed under the mordent symbol to show this alteration; this accidental applies to the lower neighbor, not to the main note. In some cases, the lower neighbor may be raised even if no accidental is printed.

The symbol for the mordent and its most typical realization are shown in Example 8A. It is also possible to interpret this symbol as a "double mordent" as in Example 8B, or even a "multi-mordent" as in 8C. Note that the mordent occurs on the beat, more like an appoggiatura than a grace note. The mordent is typically performed very quickly to give a "biting" effect ("*mordre*" is the French word for "to bite") with the main note then sustained for its duration. In a fast tempo or on a short note, the mordent may become a triplet as in Example 8D.

Example 8

Exercise 8

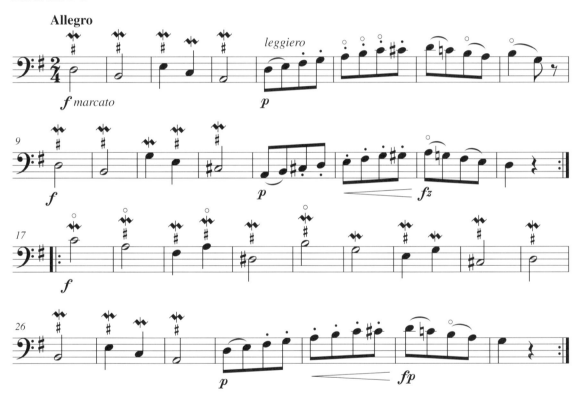

The Inverted Mordent

As the name implies, the inverted mordent is like the mordent, but in this case the main note alternates with its diatonic *upper* neighbor, be it a half or whole step. An accidental may be placed above the inverted mordent symbol to chromatically alter the pitch of the upper neighbor (see Example 9A). In Baroque music, the inverted mordent may begin with the upper neighbor (see Example 9B). When this is done, it is sometimes referred to by its German name, the *Pralltriller*. And again, like the mordent, in a fast tempo and/or on a short note the inverted mordent may be played like a triplet (Example 9B).

Example 9

Exercise 9

Lastly, it should be noted that one occasionally encounters musicians who use the terms "mordent" and "inverted mordent" opposite of how they are defined above. That is, sometimes the word "mordent" is used to denote the upper-neighbor ornament and "inverted mordent" is used to denote the lower-neighbor ornament.

The Turn

When placed directly above a note, the turn involves four notes: the upper neighbor, the written (main) note, the lower neighbor, and a return to the main note. In these cases, the first three notes are normally played quickly and on the beat, and the fourth note is sustained for the duration (Example 10A-B). On short notes (Example 10C) and/or in fast tempos (Example 10D), the turn can be played as four even notes (Example 10C-D). As with mordents, these neighbors are normally diatonic; an accidental may be placed above and/or below the turn symbol to alter the respective note (Example 10E).

Example 10

More commonly, the turn is found between notes. In these cases it involves five notes total: the written note, the upper neighbor, the written note again, the lower neighbor, and the written note yet again. The exact rhythm of the turn then becomes the question. There are so many possibilities that the rhythm of the given notes, tempo and character of the music, and the performer's taste are the best guides. Example 11 shows several common realizations.

Example 11

Exercise 10

The Inverted Turn

The inverted turn is the same as the turn except that the lower neighbor comes first, the upper neighbor later. This is usually written out in "regular" notes (Example 12A). The symbols ∾ and $ may also be used to show the inverted turn, although these are quite rare. With respect to accidentals and rhythm, the realization of the inverted turn is identical to that of the turn. (See Examples 12A and 12B, which are played the same.)

Example 12

Exercise 11

The Trill

At its core, a trill is an alternation between a note and its diatonic upper neighbor. However, this simple beginning leads to many different possibilities. The central questions for interpreting a trill are:

1) How many alternations should be played?
2) How rapid should the alternations be?
3) Should the trill begin on the written note or the upper neighbor?
4) Should the first note be performed like an appoggiatura (leaned upon and/or elongated)?
5) Should there be a *Nachschlag* at the end of the trill? If so, should the trill stop first, or go directly into the *Nachschlag?*

The trill is normally notated with the symbol *tr*; sometimes a wavy line follows the trill symbol: *tr*〰〰〰 . When this line is present, the trill should continue for the duration of the note (or the wavy line); without the wavy line, the trill may last for the entire duration of the written note or for a shorter duration.

As a general rule, in Baroque and early Classical music, the trill begins with the upper neighbor (Example 13A). In slower tempos this first note may be stressed like an appoggiatura (Example 13B); in faster tempos normally one begins trilling immediately as in Example 13A. In music written after ca.1825, trills normally begin on the written note (Example 13C) unless there is an appoggiatura or grace note(s) indicating that the trill should start otherwise (Example 13D-G).

Example 13. (Rhythmic notation is an approximation; rate and number of alternations will vary.)

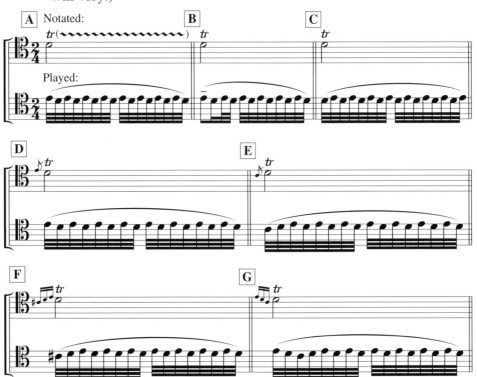

In slower tempos one usually trills more slowly; in faster tempos, more rapidly. On a very long trill, especially in Baroque music and/or near the end of cadenzas, one can begin the trill slowly and then speed up (Example 14).

Example 14. (Rhythmic notation is an approximation; rate and number of alternations will vary.)

In fast tempos and/or if the trill is on a short note, a single alternation to the upper neighbor is appropriate. Note that in these cases the trill is essentially the same as the inverted mordent. (Example 15A-B).

Example 15

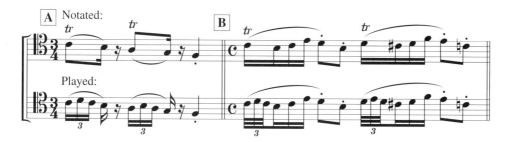

A *Nachschlag* may be added at the end of a trill; sometimes this is notated (Example 16A-B). Many times the *Nachschlag* is not notated, but may still be added; this is especially true in Baroque music and at cadences (Example 16C).

Example 16. (Rhythmic notation is an approximation; rate and number of alternations will vary.)

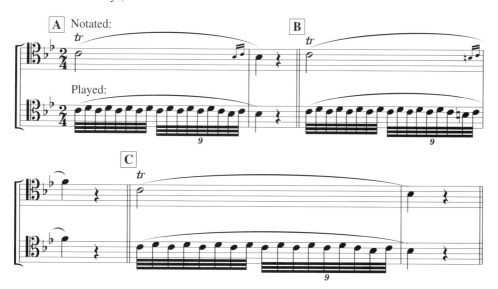

In some cases one may stop the trill before the end of the written note, sustaining the written note briefly. This is most often done on tied or dotted notes (Example 17A-D). This can also be done to help accommodate a *Nachschlag* (Example 17E).

150

Example 17. (Rhythmic notation is an approximation; rate and number of alternations will vary.)

Special mention should be made of the cadential trill. This is a melodic formula, common in Baroque and Classical music, that coincides with the V-I cadence at the end of large sections, movements, and cadenzas. It is essentially a trill on the supertonic (scale degree two, or "Re" in movable-do solfege). Even when not specifically notated, it is expected that this trill be started on the upper note (often stressed like an appoggiatura) and concluded with a *Nachschlag* or similar decoration (Example 18).

Example 18. Mozart K. 292, mvt. 2, mm. 51–52 (Notation is approximate.)

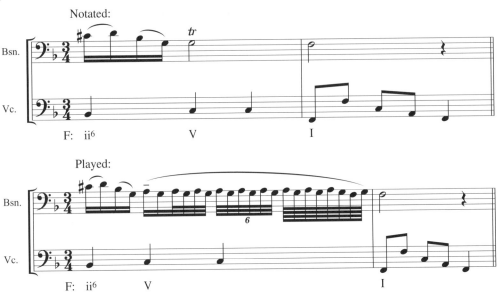

Experiment with the above possible realizations while studying Exercise 12. See Supplement Part III for additional practice with trills.

Exercise 12

Allegro moderato

152

Major and Minor Scales in All Keys*

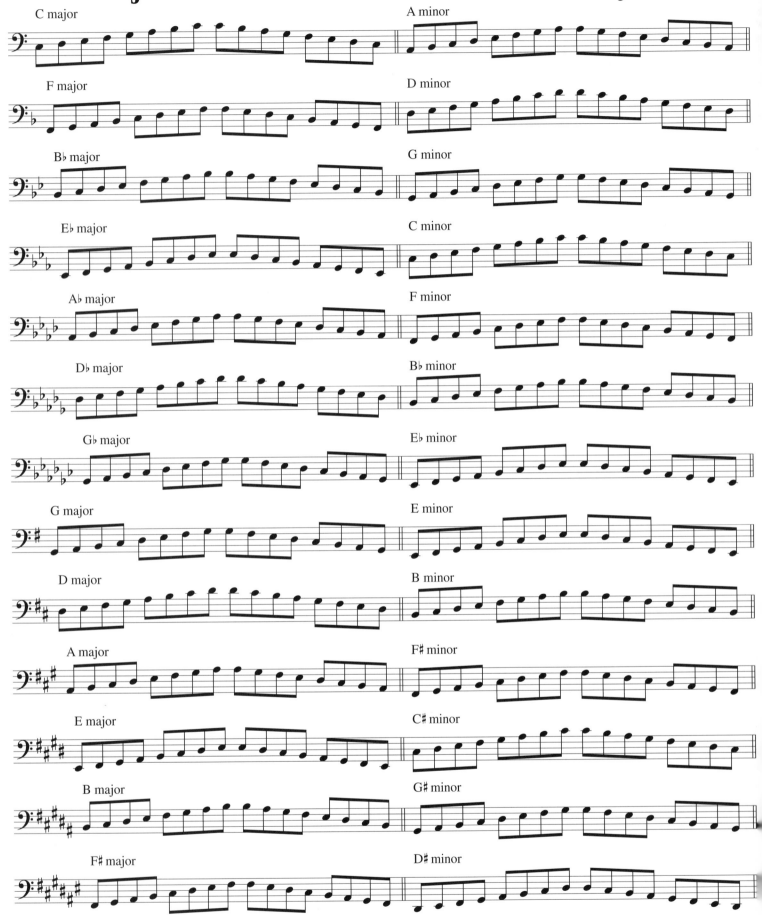

To practice the keys of C♯ major/A♯ minor (7 sharps) and C♭ major/A♭ minor (7 flats), use the first line on this page and add the applicable key signature.

*Include all three forms of minor scales in your practice:

- Natural minor – Play as written.
- Harmonic minor – The seventh note of the scale is raised one half step.
- Melodic minor – The sixth and seventh notes of the scale are raised when ascending and lowered when descending.

Supplement – Part I: Scale Studies

Scale exercises 1–31 (pp. 153–159) should be practiced in all major and minor keys. A one-octave sample of each scale is provided on p. 152.

Exercises 1–31 are written in either F Major or C Major; students should develop the ability to transpose each exercise, at sight, to the key being studied. Doing so will improve not only technique, but also musicianship skills and knowledge of music theory. The exercises should also be practiced with a variety of articulations and dynamics. When no articulations are given, play each exercise slurred, then *legato* tongued, then *staccato* tongued (or as assigned by your instructor).

One-octave range

Greater than one-octave range

Two-octave range

17.

20.

C.J.W./D.E.S.

21.

C.J.W./D.E.S.

sim.

sim.

22.

C.J.W./D.E.S.

sim.

sim.

23.

C.J.W./D.E.S.

sim.

sim.

24.

25.

26.

31.   D.E.S.

One-octave chromatic scale (transpose as needed)

32.   D.E.S.

Two-octave chromatic scale (transpose as needed)

33.   D.E.S.

Three-octave chromatic scale

34.   D.E.S.

160

Part II: Chord and Intonation Studies

As with the scale exercises, these chord studies should be practiced in all major and minor keys, and students should develop the ability to transpose these exercises at sight. The articulations used in the scale studies should be employed here as well.

The bulk of these exercises are focused upon five types of chords: the major triad, the minor triad, the dominant 7th, the half-diminished 7th chord, and the fully diminished 7th chord. An example of each is given below. Other types of 7th chords are covered in the final section.

The aim of these exercises is twofold: 1) to develop good intonation on the bassoon, and 2) to develop good technique in playing these chords. In his original edition Weissenborn discusses the need to develop good intonation, and suggests chord studies such as these as a means to that end. Those exercises that include drones are especially good for developing good intonation—practicing with the sounding drone will greatly aid this. The source of the drone can be any in-tune acoustic or electronic instrument, an electronic tuner, or pre-recorded sound.

Triads: One-octave range

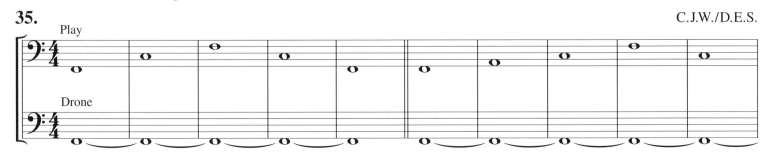

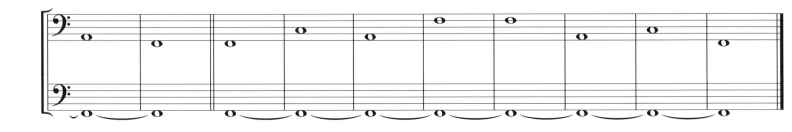

Triads: Two-octave range

38.

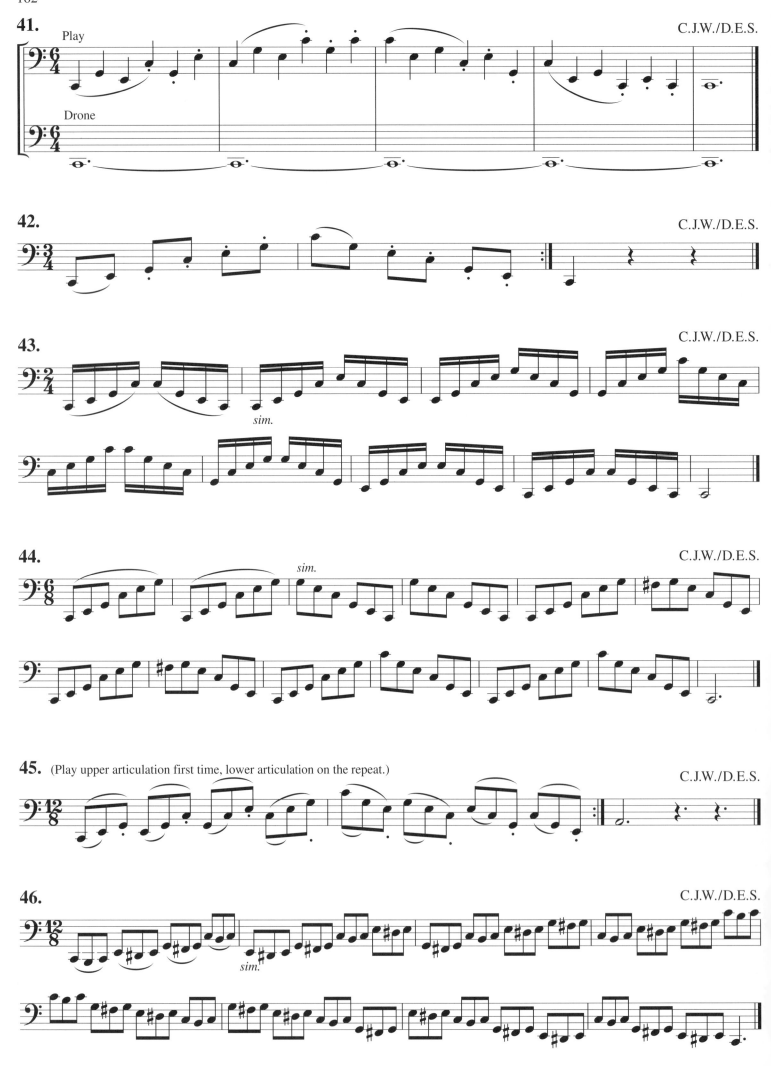

Dominant 7th: Two-octave range

47.

C.J.W./D.E.S.

48.

C.J.W./D.E.S.

sim.

49.

C.J.W./D.E.S.

sim.

50.   C.J.W./D.E.S.

51.   C.J.W./D.E.S.

52.   C.J.W./D.E.S.

53. (Play upper articulation first time, lower articulation on the repeat.)
                                                                                                       C.J.W./D.E.S.

54.   C.J.W./D.E.S.

Half-diminished 7th: Two-octave range

55.   C.J.W./D.E.S.

56.   C.J.W./D.E.S.

57.

Fully-diminished 7th: Two-octave range

58.

59.

60.

Other 7th chords: Two-octave range

61.

62.

63.

Part III: Finger and Trill Exercises

These exercises are designed to improve evenness and control of the fingers, which in turn improves general finger technique and the execution of trills. They should be transposed to cover all keys and the entire range of the instrument. Exercise 65 may be used to practice connections between any two pitches. At faster tempos, bassoonists will need to use special trill fingerings for difficult intervals; a chart of trill fingerings may be found on p. 172. Students should memorize these fingerings and practice them so that they become a useful part of their technique.

Glossary of Terms

a at, to, in, as

accelerando (accel.) becoming faster

accent (>) to emphasize or stress (a note)

Achtel eighth note (gets the beat)

adagio see *Tempos*, p. 169

ad lib. (libitum) at will or discretion, esp. regarding tempo and rubato

a due (a2) to be played by both players

agitato agitated

alla in the style or beat of

alla breve half note gets the beat

allegretto see *Tempos*, p. 169

allegro see *Tempos*, p. 169

amoroso with love (also **con amore, amorevole**)

andante, andantino see *Tempos*, p. 169

animato animated, lively (also **animando, animandosi**)

appassionato passionately

appoggiatura see Lesson XXVI

assai much, very

attacca go on to the next section without a pause

ben, bene well

binary form a two-part musical form with a strong cadence at the end of each section:
‖ A | B ‖

breath mark see Lesson IV

breve (𝄺) a note equal to two whole notes (eight quarter notes)

brio spirit

brioso spirited

caesura (//) a silent pause with a stopping of the tempo

calando becoming softer and slower

canon a composition for two or more parts in which the first voice is strictly imitated by the other voices

cantabile singing (also **cantando**)

canzonetta a short song

capriccioso capriciously (also **capricciosamente**)

coda closing section of a composition

comodo comfortable, easy, especially in regard to tempo (also **comodamente**)

compound ternary form a ternary form in which each main section is divided into two subsections:
‖ A1 | A2 ‖ B1 | B2 ‖ A1 | A2 ‖

con with (also **col, colla, colle**)

crescendo (cresc.) becoming louder

da from

da Capo (D.C.) from the beginning

dal Segno (D.S.) from the sign

decrescendo (decresc.) becoming softer

di of

diminuendo (dim. or dimin.) becoming softer

dolce sweetly, softly (also **dolcemente**)

dolcissimo very sweetly

e and

embellishments see Lesson XXVI

energico energetically (also **con energia**)

espressivo (espress.) expressively (also **con espressione**)

fermata (𝄐) a sign indicating that a note or rest should be held longer than its rhythmic value

fifth an interval of five notes; i.e., C4 to G4

Fine the end

flick keys see Lesson XII.b

form the organization of sections in a piece of music, represented by letters that depict similar and contrasting sections: AB, ABA, AABA, etc.

forte (f) and related see *Dynamics*, p. 169

fortepiano (fp) see *Dynamics*, p. 169

forza force, strength
  con tutta forza with all your force

forzando (fz) forcing, accented

fourth an interval of four notes; i.e., C4 to F4

funebre funereal

fuoco fire

giocoso   jocose, humorous

gioioso   joyous

giusto   just, precise, in strict time

grace note   see Lesson XXVI

grandioso   grandiose

grave   see *Tempos*, p. 169

grazia   grace

grazioso   graceful

half hole   see Lesson XI

interval   the distance between any two pitches

inverted mordent   see Lesson XXVI

langsam   slow

largo and related   see *Tempos*, p. 169

legato   smoothly, no separation between notes

legg(i)ero   lightly

lento   see *Tempos*, p. 169

l'istesso   the same (tempo)

loco   in the octave written

ma   but

maestoso   majestically

marcato   marked, accented, separated

marcia   march

marziale   martial, march-like

mässig(es)   moderate, moderately

meno _____   less
(**meno** alone = **meno mosso**, i.e., slower)

mesto   sadly, mournfully

mezzo   medium, half

minuetto   an elegant dance in three

mit vollem Ton   with full tone

moderato   see *Tempos*, p. 169

molto   much, very

mordent   see Lesson XXVI

morendo   dying away

mosso   moved, agitated
(**più mosso** = faster)

moto   motion

Nachschlag   see Lesson XXVI

non   non-, not

octave   an interval of eight notes, i.e., C3 to C4

ossia   or, as in an alternate passage

ottava (*8va*)   play an octave higher

patetico   with great emotion

pesante   heavy, with emphasis

(a) piacere   at your pleasure, esp. regarding tempo
and rubato

piano (*p*) and related   see *Dynamics*, p. 169

più _____   more
(**più** alone = **più mosso**, i.e., faster)

poco   little

poco a poco   little by little, gradually

Polonaise   festive Polish dance in triple meter

pomposo   pompous, grand

portamento   sliding or carrying from one note to
the next

portato (.⌢.)   articulation between legato and staccato;
slightly and gently separated

presto and related   see *Tempos*, p. 169

quasi   similar to, in the style of

rallentando (**rall.**)   becoming slower

rinforzando (*rf*)   reinforced, accented

risoluto   resolute

ritardando (**rit.**)   gradually slower

ritenuto (**riten.**)   held back, suddenly slower

rounded binary form   a two-part musical form in
which some or all of the music from the A section
reappears at the end of the B section without a strong
cadence between the two:
‖ A | B A ‖

ruhig(e)   peaceful, calmly

scherzando   playfully

schnell   fast, quick

segue   go on without interruption

sehr   very

semplice simply, plainly

sempre always, continuously

senza without

sforzando (*sf*, *sfz*) with force, accented

simile, simili (sim.) in a similar manner

sin' (sino) until

smorzando dying away

soli a featured passage played in unison by more than one person

solo a featured passage played by only one person

sonoro sonorously, with full tone

sostenuto sustained

speaker keys see Lesson XII.b

spiritoso spirited (also **con spirito**)

staccato detached, separated

stringendo becoming faster

subito (sub.) suddenly

tacet silent; i.e., this instrument/voice does not play in this section/movement

tanto so/too much
   (**non tanto** = not so/too much)

tempo primo return to original tempo (also **a tempo**)

tenuto (ten.) held, sustained

ternary form a three-part musical form (usually ‖ A | B | A ‖) that includes a strong cadence at the end of each section

third an interval of three notes; i.e., C4 to E4

tranquillo tranquil, quiet, calm

trill see Lesson XXVI

trio a contrasting middle section in a composition (most often: minuet – trio – minuet)

triplet (⌐3⌐) a rhythm dividing a beat into three equal parts that is normally divided into two parts

troppo too much (**ma non troppo** = but not too much)

turn see Lesson XXVI

tutti all play

un a, an, one

vent keys see Lesson XII.b

Viertel quarter note (gets the beat)

vivace fast, lively

vivo lively, briskly (also **vivamente**)

volti subito (V.S.) turn page quickly

Walzertempo waltz tempo

wedge see Lesson IV

Zeitmass tempo

Tempos (from slow to fast)

grave very slow, serious, grave

largo broad

larghetto slightly faster than largo

lento slow

adagio at ease, slow

andante walking, somewhat slow

andantino* slightly faster than andante

moderato moderately

allegretto slightly slower than allegro

allegro quick, happy, cheerful

vivace lively

presto very fast

prestissimo as fast as possible

   *In some older music, **andantino** was used to mean slightly slower than andante

Dynamics (from soft to loud)

ppp (**pianississimo**) very, very soft

pp (**pianissimo**) very soft

p (**piano**) soft

mp (**mezzopiano**) medium soft

mf (**mezzoforte**) medium loud

f (**forte**) loud

ff (**fortissimo**) very loud

fff (**fortississimo**) very, very loud

fp (**fortepiano**) begin *f* and immediately drop to *p*

Fingering Chart

This chart includes fingerings for every note introduced in this book. These are the same fingerings provided in the Practical Exercises; they are compiled here for easy reference.

Tone holes that are blackened are to be covered; keys that are blackened are to be depressed. Gray tone holes and keys are optional. When more then one fingering is given, the first is the most commonly used or the one recommended by this author as a standard fingering. Other fingerings given may also be used as a standard fingering or for special uses as described. See the lesson in which the note is first introduced for additional information. *Refer to p. 15 for a diagram of key names.*

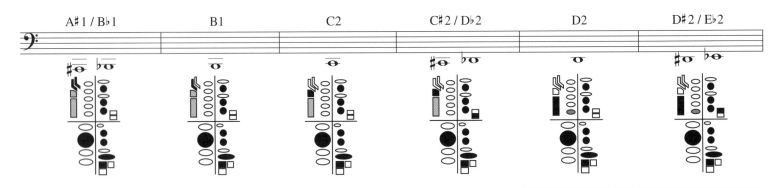

Note that the Low B Key automatically closes the Low C and Low D keys, and that the Low C Key automatically closes the Low D Key.

Note that the Low E key automatically closes the whisper key. If D2 or D#2/E♭2 is followed by a lower note, keep your thumb off the whisper key, close to the Low C key. If followed by a higher note, keep your thumb on the Low D Key and the whisper key.

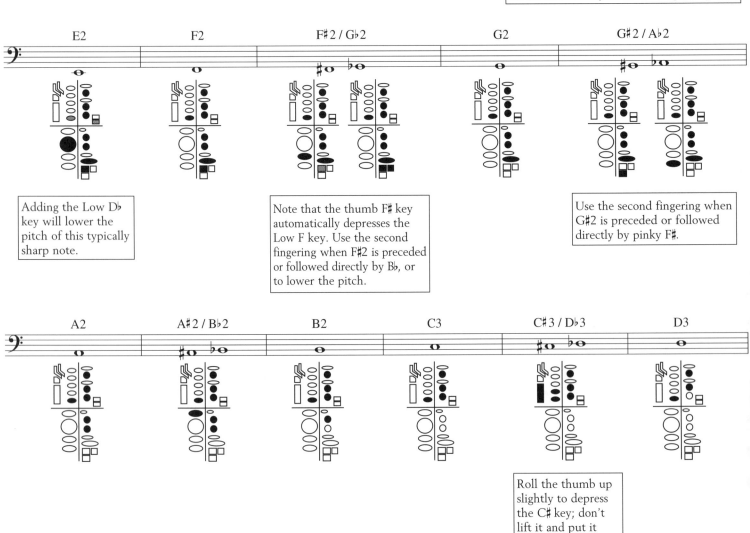

Adding the Low D♭ key will lower the pitch of this typically sharp note.

Note that the thumb F# key automatically depresses the Low F key. Use the second fingering when F#2 is preceded or followed directly by B♭, or to lower the pitch.

Use the second fingering when G#2 is preceded or followed directly by pinky F#.

Roll the thumb up slightly to depress the C# key; don't lift it and put it back down.

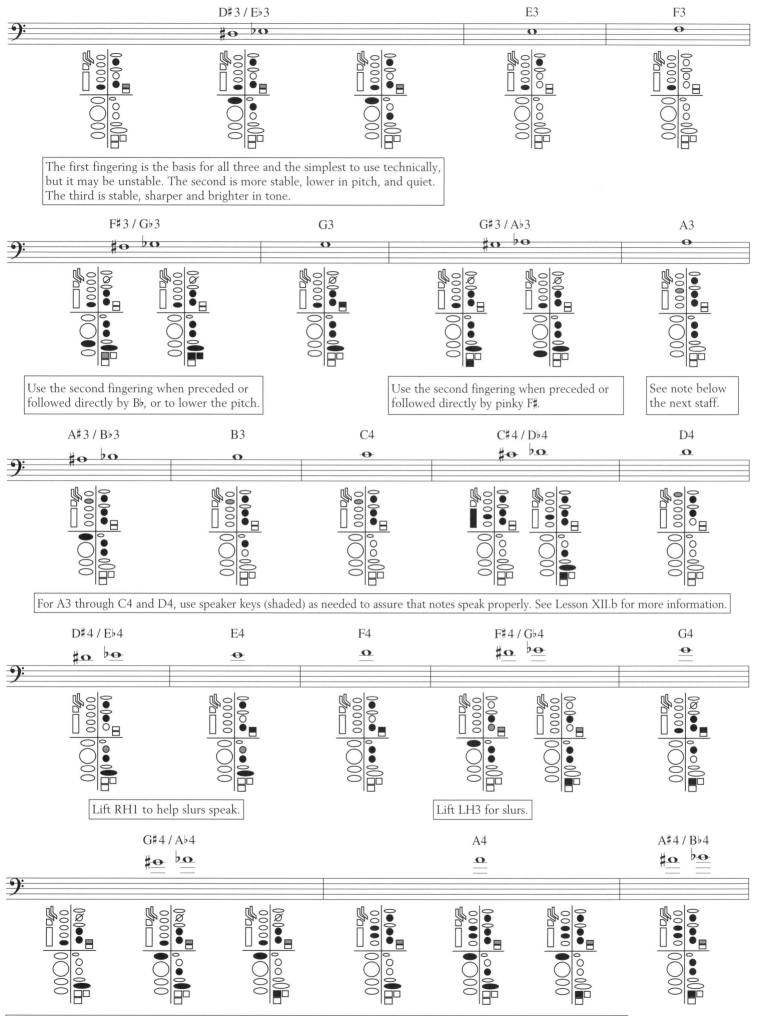

D#3 / E♭3   E3   F3

The first fingering is the basis for all three and the simplest to use technically, but it may be unstable. The second is more stable, lower in pitch, and quiet. The third is stable, sharper and brighter in tone.

F#3 / G♭3   G3   G#3 / A♭3   A3

Use the second fingering when preceded or followed directly by B♭, or to lower the pitch.

Use the second fingering when preceded or followed directly by pinky F#.

See note below the next staff.

A#3 / B♭3   B3   C4   C#4 / D♭4   D4

For A3 through C4 and D4, use speaker keys (shaded) as needed to assure that notes speak properly. See Lesson XII.b for more information.

D#4 / E♭4   E4   F4   F#4 / G♭4   G4

Lift RH1 to help slurs speak.

Lift LH3 for slurs.

G#4 / A♭4   A4   A#4 / B♭4

For both A♭4 and A4, any of the three given fingerings can be used as a standard fingering. The first is perhaps the most common. The second is flatter in pitch and fuller in tone. The third can help alleviate fingering difficulties in this register.

Trill Fingerings

This chart includes the fingerings to be used on trills for which it is not possible/practical to use the two standard fingerings. Some of these fingerings may also be used to alleviate technical difficulties in passages other than trills, but this should be done sparingly. When more than one set of fingerings is given for a trill, it is recommended that you try all the given fingerings to find which one works best for you in the given passage. It is almost always advisable that the first note of a trill be fingered with a standard fingering, switching to the trill fingering for the remaining notes in the trill.

This list is by no means comprehensive. It does provide common solutions to difficult trills within the range of this book (B♭1 to B♭4). If a trill is not listed here, it is either playable with standard fingerings or it is not possible/ practical to do on the bassoon. If necessary, consult one of the sources listed in the bibliography. Bassoonists spend a lifetime finding new fingerings for trills and difficult passsages. (Note: Most, if not all, of these fingerings are common knowledge among professional bassoonists. In cases where I learned of a fingering from a specific identifiable source, I've credited that source below the fingering.)

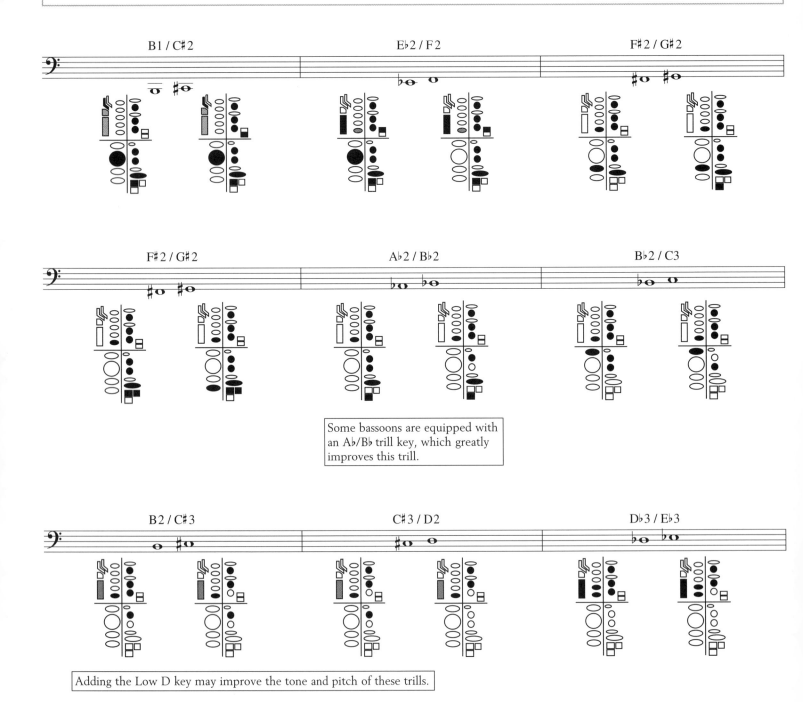

Some bassoons are equipped with an A♭/B♭ trill key, which greatly improves this trill.

Adding the Low D key may improve the tone and pitch of these trills.

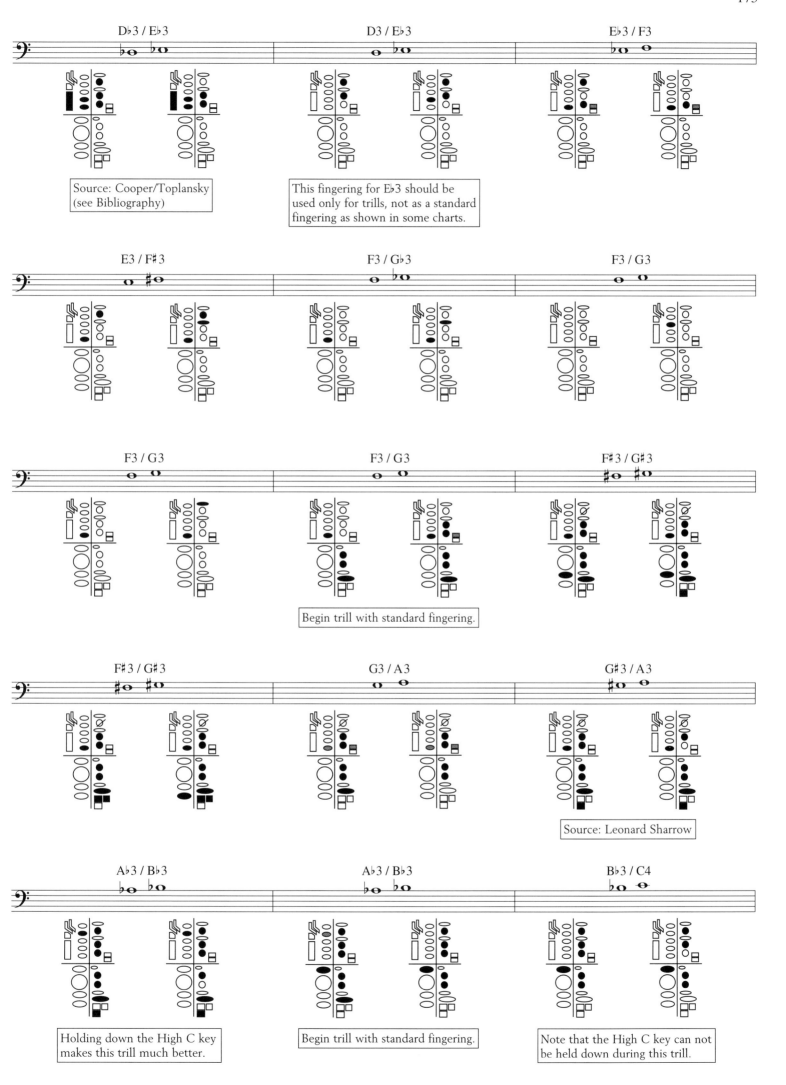

174

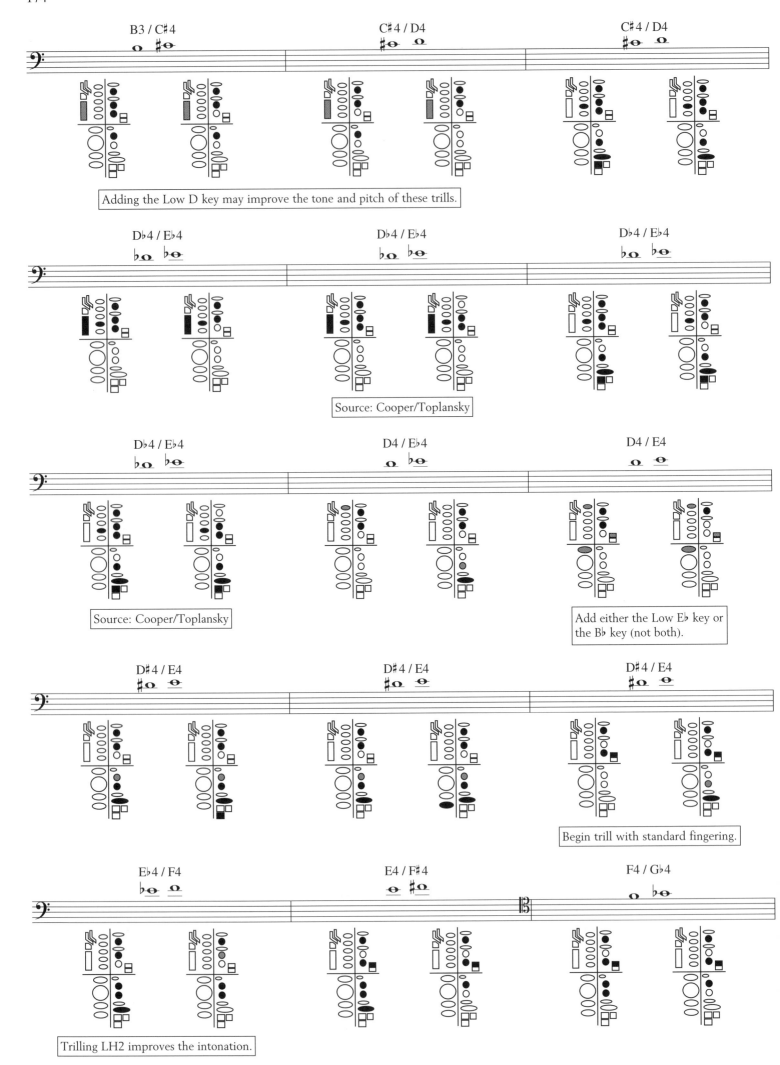

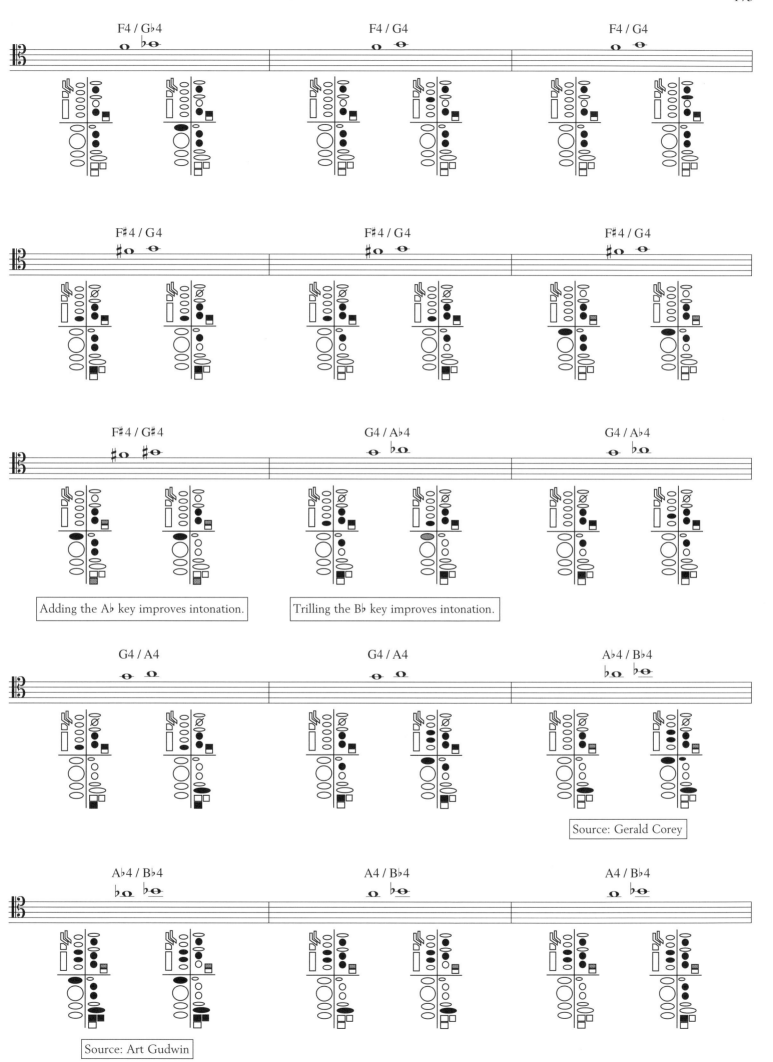

Adding the A♭ key improves intonation.

Trilling the B♭ key improves intonation.

Source: Gerald Corey

Source: Art Gudwin

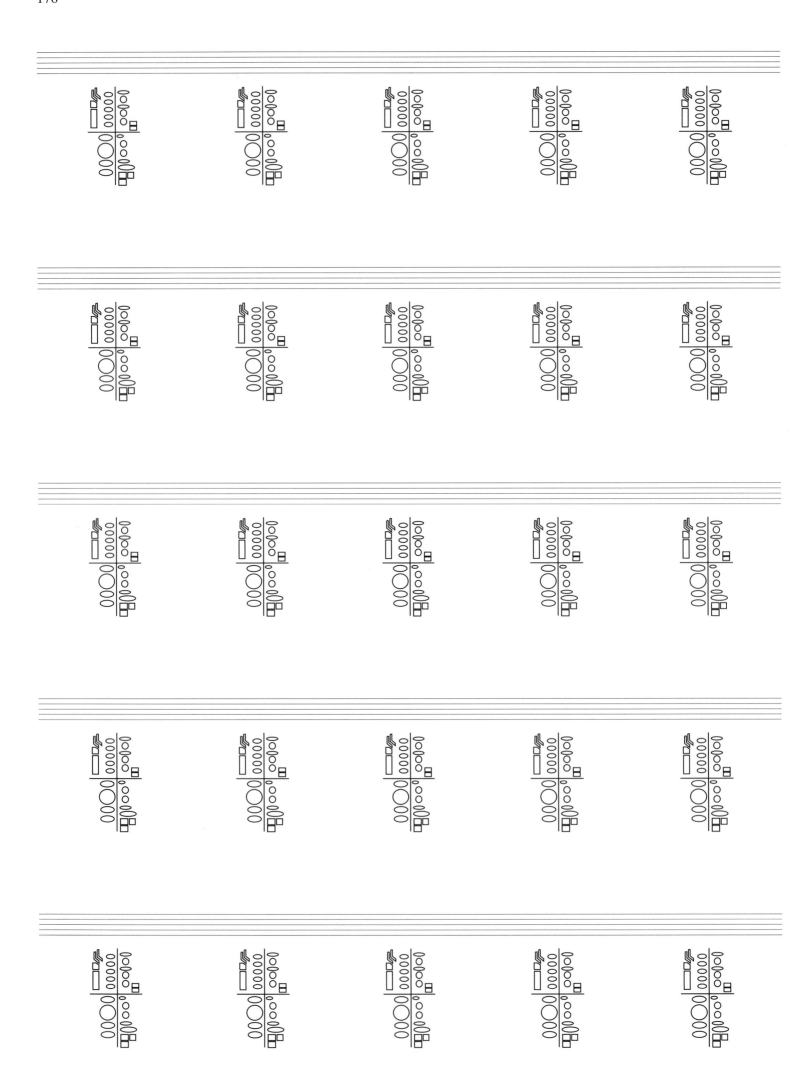

About the Author

Doug Spaniol is Professor of Music in the School of Music at Butler University's Jordan College of the Arts, where he teaches bassoon and courses in reed-making, pedagogy, theory, and chamber music. In the summers, he serves as instructor of bassoon at the world-renowned Interlochen Arts Camp. He was previously a member of the faculty at Valdosta State University and has twice served as visiting professor at The Ohio State University.

His bassoon students have enjoyed remarkable success, including being named a winner of the Yamaha Young Performing Artists Competition, and placing in the International Double Reed Society's Young Artists Competition and Meg Quigley Vivaldi Competition. Other competition successes have lead to concerto performances with the Indianapolis Symphony Orchestra, the Butler Symphony Orchestra, Interlochen's World Youth Symphony Orchestra, and the Kokomo Symphony Orchestra. In addition, his students have performed on National Public Radio's *From the Top*, been offered scholarships and graduate assistantships to America's finest music schools, and have performed with the Indianapolis Symphony Orchestra, Louisville Orchestra, Indianapolis Chamber Orchestra, Sinfonia da Camera, and many other ensembles.

As a Fulbright Scholar, Dr. Spaniol spent the first half of 2012 in England teaching at the University of York and furthering his research and restoration of Weissenborn's pedagogical bassoon works. This resulted in a new edition of Weissenborn's Advanced Studies, Op. 8, No. 2 (which for the first time makes available all 60 of the studies as Weissenborn originally intended), and an upcoming edition of Weissenborn's complete works for bassoon and piano (including three that have never been published). Previously he was named a Marshall Scholar and subsequently studied at the Royal Northern College of Music, where he was awarded the prestigious postgraduate diploma in performance.

Dr. Spaniol has presented masterclasses at the Royal Academy of Music (London), St. Petersburg (Russia) Conservatory, Indiana University, and for the Music for All/Bands of America National Festival, among many others. He frequently appears as a performer/presenter at music education conferences and the annual conferences of the International Double Reed Society. He also served for six years as Bassoon Chair for the IDRS's Fernand Gillet – Hugo Fox Competition.

As a performer, Dr. Spaniol has appeared as concerto soloist with Sinfonia da Camera, the St. Petersburg Classical Symphony Orchestra, Solisti St. Petersburg, the Central Ohio Symphony Orchestra, the Philharmonic Orchestra of Indianapolis, and Butler's Symphonic Wind Ensemble and Jordan Sinfonia. He can be heard as soloist on two CDs: *Bassoon with a View* (Innova 520) and *Frank Felice: Sidewalk Music* (Capstone CPS-8707). As a member of *Arbitrio* (with Alicia Cordoba Tait, oboe, and Bradley Haag, piano) he has performed throughout the Midwest, in St. Petersburg, Russia, and Buenos Aires, Argentina, and recorded a CD for Centaur Records (CRC 3013). As principal bassoonist of Sinfonia da Camera, Dr. Spaniol has toured England, been heard on NPR's *Performance Today*, and appears on CDs on Albany and Zephyr Records and the *Classical Music for Dummies* CD.

Dr. Spaniol earned a Doctor of Musical Arts degree from The Ohio State University and Master of Music and Bachelor of Music degrees from the University of Illinois. His bassoon teachers include Christopher Weait, William Waterhouse, and E. Sanford Berry. A Yamaha Artist/Clinician, Dr. Spaniol plays a Yamaha YFG-811 bassoon.